Simple Tarts

Simple Tarts

Sweet and savoury recipes
for all occasions

Elizabeth Wolf-Cohen

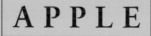

A QUINTET BOOK

Published by The Apple Press
6 Blundell Street
London N7 9BH

ISBN 1-85076-687-8

This book was designed and produced by
Quintet Publishing Limited
6 Blundell Street
London N7 9BH

Creative Director: Richard Dewing
Designer: Isobel Gillan
Senior Editor: Anna Briffa
Home Economist: Elizabeth Wolf-Cohen
Editor: Barbara Croxford
Photographer: Tim Hill
Assistant Home Economist: Zöe Kean

Typeset in Great Britain by
Central Southern Typesetters, Eastbourne
Manufactured in Malaysia by C.H. Colourscan Sdn Bhd
Printed in China by Leefung-Asco Printers Ltd

CONTENTS

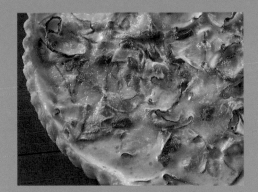

INTRODUCTION

Simple Tarts is a book for pastry lovers and those who love simple fresh food. Tarts have an appealing freshness which underlines a tasty filling that can be sweet or savoury, and light or filling and substantial.

Tarts, or open pastry cases, play a part in many culinary traditions, but have played a very important part in British, American and French cuisines. Tarts can easily form the basis of simple desserts such as a fresh berry tart, or an elaborate sweet such as the Mocha Mousse Slice. Leek and Onion Tartlets or Mussel and Leek Tart make a substantial main course. In fact, tarts make an ideal showcase for an amazing variety of foods.

Most of these tarts are easy to prepare and, with a little forethought, can be put together quickly. Remember pastry can be bought from supermarkets and home-made pastry freezes well, so make it in batches and freeze ahead. Fillings can be assembled in no time, so use your imagination and enjoy the treat of a simple tart made with delicious tender pastry, warm from the oven.

Every cook I know aspires to make light, tender flaky pastry. There are a few basic commandments that must always be obeyed, regardless of what kind of pastry you choose:

● Chill all the ingredients. (My pastry teacher used to keep a bag of flour in the freezer!)

● Work as quickly as possible and, unless you are one of those natural born pastry makers, use a pastry blender (instead of two knives) or use the ideal tool – a food processor.

● Chill the pastry after every stage of making and assembling: chill after patting into a disc and after rolling out and lining the tart or pie tin. Do not be tempted to cheat – your pastry will shrink unevenly.

● Pastry likes a hot oven; butter-rich pastries and puff pastry especially require a hot blast of heat to seal the pastry and release the steam. If longer cooking is required for a filling, the temperature can be reduced so the pastry does not burn.

THE INGREDIENTS

Most kinds of pastry are made with a combination of flour, fat and a liquid to bind. The texture, flavour and colour of the resulting pastry will vary tremendously depending on the proportions and types of ingredients used.

Flour

Plain flour is used throughout this book. Even the same brand of flour can vary from season to season, depending on humidity or how long it has been stored, however, so the amount of liquid necessary to bind the pastry will always vary; ⅛ teaspoon baking powder can be added to 150g/5½oz flour to achieve a lighter result. Wholemeal or rye flour can replace some of the white flour in savoury pastry, but produces a heavier result. Use equal amounts or more white flour proportionally to wholemeal or other flours for easier handling. Please note that it is always essential to be consistent when using either metric or imperial, and not to mix the two.

Fat

Lard was probably the first fat used in pastry making, but has fallen out of favour for health reasons. It does make a very short and tender pastry, but has a distinctive taste. My choice is butter. Pure butter gives pastry a rich flavour and colour and a crisp texture, but it can be difficult to handle. Most bakers use a combination of butter or hard margarine (not the soft tub variety) and white vegetable fat to achieve a balance of good buttery colour and flavour with the short flaky texture provided by white fat. I use unsalted butter because it has a lower water content and the amount of salt can be more easily controlled. Experiment until you find your own preference.

The normal proportion of fat to flour is usually half fat to flour (i.e. one part fat to two parts flour), although some rich European-style pastries, such as *pâte sucrée* have a higher percentage of fat. The more fat the dough has, the more difficult it will be to handle, so be sure the dough is chilled at all stages of handling.

Liquid

Most pastry is bound with water, although milk or other liquids can be used. Normal tart pastry uses about 1 teaspoon of water per 25g/1oz flour; this varies if eggs or an egg yolk is added. The water should be iced water so it does not melt or soften the fat(s). Too much water will make a sticky pastry, which is difficult to handle and produces tough pastry. Be careful when using a food processor, since the mixture can form into a pastry before the correct quantity of liquid has been added. This can produce a dough that is too short and is difficult to handle and results in a brittle, too crumbly pastry. Many recipes call for an egg yolk mixed with water to a certain measure. This adds a golden colour and helps to bind the pastry. Sometimes a little juice is added for flavour, but be careful as certain juices, such as lemon, contain a high proportion of acid, which can shorten the pastry too much for easy handling. A little grated orange or lemon rind should add just the right kind of flavour. Flavourings such as vanilla, almond or lemon can be used to enhance the chosen fillings, as can spices such as cinnamon, nutmeg, ginger or cardamom.

Eggs

Eggs are added to pastry for richness in texture and flavour, and because they help bind all the ingredients. Normally only the yolk is used and, for a very rich biscuit-like pastry used in some European-style tarts, yolks are used without any other liquid.

Sugar

Sugar is used both to sweeten the final pastry and create a crisper texture. A tea-spoon or two is often added even to savoury doughs, because the sugar helps the pastry to colour and gives a more golden look. Caster sugar or icing sugar is usually used because these types dissolve more quickly than granulated. Granulated sugar can be used but can result in a crunchy texture not always desired.

Commercial Pastry

Excellent quality shortcrust, puff pastry and phyllo pastry can be purchased in supermarkets, and all give good reliable results. Puff pastry is available chilled or frozen and gives excellent results. Look for the all-butter variety since the flavour is superior. Phyllo pastry is also available chilled or frozen and is a great freezer stand-by. These paper-thin sheets of pastry need to be defrosted before being carefully unwrapped. Because the thin layers dry so quickly, they should be covered with a damp tea towel when working.

chapter one

MAKING PASTRY

Although many good-quality, ready-made pastries are available, there is nothing quite as satisfying as making your own. The method for making Basic Shortcrust Pastry is easy to follow and, once mastered, can be adapted for both sweet and savoury tarts simply by adding a few extra ingredients.

BASIC SHORTCRUST PASTRY (Pâte Brisée)

Brisée in French means broken. In this pastry the flour and fats are "broken together", or cut in. After adding the liquid, the pastry is blended until the mixture begins to bind together. If the pastry becomes sticky at any stage, refrigerate until it is easy to handle. This recipe should produce a firm, yet flaky crust which can support a filling but is still tender. Sifting flour is not absolutely necessary, but it can help lighten the pastry if you use the hand method.

Ingredients

- For a 23–25-cm/9–10-in tart tin

- 180g/6¼oz plain flour
- ½ tsp salt
- 1 tsp caster sugar, optional
- 90g/3oz cold unsalted butter, cut into small pieces
- 25g/1oz cold margarine or white vegetable fat, cut into small pieces
- 2-4 tbsp iced water

Hand Method

1 Into a large bowl, sift the flour, salt and sugar if using. Sprinkle the pieces of butter and margarine or white vegetable fat over the flour mixture. Using a pastry blender or two knives scissor-fashion, cut in the fat until the mixture forms coarse crumbs. Do not over-work, as this causes a tough crust.

2 Sprinkle about 2 tablespoons of the water over the flour-crumb mixture and toss lightly with a fork. Gather the parts of pastry that have bound together to one side of the bowl. Add a little more water to any dry crumbs and toss again.

3 Gather the pastry into a rough ball and turn on to a sheet of cling film. Using the cling film as a guide, lightly press the pastry into a disc shape and flatten slightly. Wrap the pastry tightly and refrigerate for at least 1 hour or overnight.

Food Processor Method

If you have warm hands, are working in hot weather, tend to have a heavy touch or just have not got the knack, the food processor should be the answer to your prayers. Used carefully, it produces perfect pastry every time; just take care not to over-process. Although shortcrust pastry is easily made by hand, the sweeter pastries do benefit from the food processor method. The more sugar and fat added to the pastry, the more difficult it is to handle.

1 Put the flour, salt and sugar in the bowl of a food processor fitted with the metal blade. Process for 5–7 seconds just to blend. Sprinkle the pieces of butter and margarine or white vegetable fat over the surface and process for 10–15 seconds until the mixture resembles coarse crumbs.

2 Sprinkle about 2 tablespoons of the water over the flour-crumb mixture and, using the pulse button, process the mixture until the pastry just begins to hold together, 10–15 seconds. DO NOT OVERPROCESS. Test the pastry by pinching a piece between your fingers: if it is still too crumbly, add more water, little by little, and pulse again until the pastry begins to stick together in clumps. Do not allow the pastry to form into a ball or add too much water because the baked pastry will be tough. Turn the pastry on to a sheet of cling film and continue with step 3 on page 9.

ROLLING AND SHAPING THE PASTRY

If the pastry has been refrigerated for more than an hour, allow it to soften slightly at room temperature for about 10 minutes.

To Form a Pastry Circle

1 Unwrap the pastry and place on a lightly floured surface. Using a lightly floured rolling pin, press parallel grooves into the pastry. Turn the pastry 45°, flouring the surface underneath and press more parallel grooves. Continue rotating and pressing the pastry, being careful the pastry does not stick, until it is about 1cm/½in thick. This method avoids overworking the pastry before actually rolling it.

2 Beginning from the centre, lightly roll out the pastry to the far edge, but do not actually roll over the edge. Return to the centre and roll to the near edge, but do not roll over the edge. Turn the pastry 45° and continue rolling until it is about 0.3cm/⅛in thick and forms a 30-cm/12-in round. Do not allow the pastry to stick to the work surface; lightly flour the surface and rolling pin as necessary, using a small pastry brush to remove any excess flour from the pastry.

> **TIP:** *To freeze rolled-out pastry, carefully slide on to a flat baking sheet and freeze, uncovered, until very firm. Remove from freezer and slide on to freezer paper, wrap well and re-freeze, with paper in between each layer. Wrap tightly and store in the freezer. Defrost in the refrigerator overnight or at room temperature several hours before using.*

3 If the pastry is tender or tears, patch it with a small piece of moistened pastry. As the pastry circle enlarges, fold it in half or into quarters to rotate and dust with flour to avoid stretching it.

To Form a Square or Rectangle

Proceed as for rolling out a circle but rotate the pastry 90° rather than 45° when making the grooves. This will cause the pastry to elongate to fill a square or rectangular tin.

Lining a Tart Tin

The traditional tart tin is shallow with no rim. It usually has a fluted side and remove-able base that gives the characteristic edge and allows the side of the tin to be removed for presentation without disturbing the base of the tart. Flan rings are generally smooth-sided rings which are set on a heavy baking sheet to form its base; these are generally used by professionals. The best tins are dull metal or non-stick since shiny metal reflects the heat and prevents the crust from browning properly. Butter-rich pastry does not generally stick, but I like to lightly spray the tart tin with a vegetable cooking spray. Alternatively, brush the bottom and side of the tart tin with a little oil.

1 To transfer rolled-out pastry to a tart tin, set the rolling pin on the near edge of the pastry round, square, or rectangle. Fold the edge of the pastry over the rolling pin, then continue to roll pastry loosely around the pin.

2 Hold far edge of pastry and rolling pin over far edge of the tart tin and gently unroll the pastry, allowing it to settle into the tin without stretching or pulling.

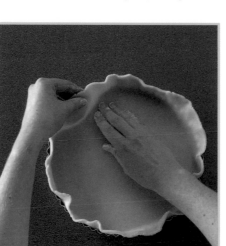

3 Using floured fingertips, lift outside edge of pastry and ease into bottom and side of tin, allowing excess pastry to overhang the edge. Smooth the pastry on to the bottom of the tin and press the overhang down slightly towards the centre of the tin, making the top edge thicker.

4 Roll the rolling pin over the edge, cutting off any excess pastry and flattening the top edge. Press the thickened top edge against the side of the tin to form a stand-up edge. This makes the edge slightly thicker and higher, reinforcing the side of the pastry case. Prick the bottom of the pastry with a fork and, if you like, crimp or decorate the edge. Refrigerate 1 hour or freeze for 20 minutes.

Lining Tartlet Tins

For very small tartlet tins (less than 5cm/2in), arrange the tins on the work surface close together and unroll the rolled-out pastry over them, loosely draping the pastry into them. Roll the rolling pin over them to cut off the excess pastry, then, using a floured thumb, press the pastry on to the bottom and up the side of the tins. Prick the bottoms with a fork. For larger tartlets, I prefer to follow the steps for lining a round tart tin, since this gives adequate pastry and a firm high edge to support any filling.

Blind Baking

Blind baking is a method of prebaking a pastry case, either partially or completely, to prevent the pastry from becoming soggy and to ensure the base cooks evenly.

1 Cut out a circle of greaseproof paper or foil about 7.5cm/3in larger than the tart tin. Fold the paper or foil in half and lay it across the centre of the pastry-lined tart tin. Unfold it and press on to the bottom, into the edge and up the side of the pastry.

2 Fill the paper- or foil-lined tart case with dried beans, rice or pastry weights, being careful to spread them evenly over the bottom and up the side. The dried beans, rice or pastry weights can be cooled and saved to use again.

3 To partially blind bake pastry: bake in a 200°C/400°F/Gas 6 oven for 15–20 minutes until the pastry is set and the rim looks dry and slightly golden. Carefully remove to a heatproof surface and remove the paper or foil and beans. The pastry case can now be filled and the baking completed.

4 To completely blind bake pastry: bake in a 200°C/400°F/Gas 6 oven for 10 minutes. Remove to a heatproof surface and carefully remove the paper or foil and beans. Gently prick the pastry bottom again with a fork and continue baking for 5–10 minutes until golden. The bottom should look dry and set. Cool completely on a wire rack before filling.

RICH SHORTCRUST PASTRY (*Pâte Brisée Riche*)

Ingredients
- For a 25-cm/10-in tart tin

- 180g/6¼oz plain flour
- ½ tsp salt
- 115g/4oz cold unsalted butter, cut into small pieces
- 1 egg yolk beaten with 2 tbsp iced water

Proceed as for Basic Shortcrust Pastry (*Pâte Brisée*), using the beaten egg yolk and water to bind.

RICH HERB SHORTCRUST PASTRY

This tender green-flecked pastry is ideal for savoury tarts. Vary the herbs to suit the filling and your taste.

Ingredients
- For a 25-cm/10-in tart tin

- 100g/6¼oz plain flour
- ½ tsp salt
- 115g/4oz cold unsalted butter
- ½ tsp fresh thyme leaves or ¼ tsp dried thyme
- ½ tsp fresh oregano or marjoram chopped or ¼ tsp dried oregano or marjoram
- 2 tbsp chopped chives
- 1 tbsp fresh parsley, chopped
- 4–6 fresh basil leaves, torn into small pieces
- 1 egg yolk beaten with 2 tbsp iced water

Prepare as for Rich Shortcrust Pastry, adding the herbs when the flour and butter have been combined to form coarse crumbs, and before adding the water.

LIGHT WHOLEMEAL PASTRY

This wholemeal crust remains light and flaky by substituting less than half the white flour for wholemeal. Substitute 15g/½oz of white vegetable fat for that amount of butter if you would like to produce a very flaky pastry.

Ingredients

- For a 25-cm/10-in tart tin

- 115g/4oz plain flour
- 75g/2⅔oz wholemeal flour
- ½ tsp salt
- 45g/1½oz cold unsalted butter, cut into small pieces
- 15g/½oz white vegetable fat or hard margarine
- 1 egg yolk beaten with 2 tbsp iced water

Proceed as for Basic Shortcrust Pastry, combining the two flours and salt before cutting in the fats.

BASIC SWEET PASTRY (*Pâte Sucrée*)

Pâte sucrée, "sweetened pastry", is made in the same way as *pâte brisée,* but contains more sugar and is generally bound with egg yolks or a combination of egg yolks and water. I use icing sugar because it dissolves instantly, but caster sugar can also be used. These additions make the pastry sweeter and a little crisper than ordinary shortcrust pastry, which is ideal for dessert and fruit tarts. After the pastry is formed, it is lightly kneaded by a process the French call *fresage* where the heel of the hand blends the pastry until it is soft and pliable. The addition of sugar and egg yolk makes the pastry softer and more difficult to handle, so be sure to chill all the ingredients and work quickly. However, because this is a soft pastry, it is easy to patch; just press any tears together – they will not show. This pastry can be made by hand by following the instructions for Basic Shortcrust Pastry, but I prefer to use the food processor and find the results equally successful.

Ingredients

- For a 23–25-cm/9–10-in tart tin or ten 7.5-cm/3-in tartlet tins

- 150g/5½oz plain flour
- ½ tsp salt
- 3–4 tbsp icing sugar
- 115g/4oz cold unsalted butter, cut into small pieces
- 2 egg yolks beaten with 2 tbsp iced water and ½ tsp vanilla essence (optional)

1 Put the flour, salt and sugar in the bowl of a food processor, fitted with the metal blade. Process for 5–7 seconds. Sprinkle the butter over the flour mixture and process for 10–15 seconds until the mixture resembles coarse crumbs. Pulse 2–3 times more if the crumbs are not evenly distributed.

2 With the machine running, pour the yolk-water mixture through the feed tube and process just until the pastry begins to hold together. DO NOT OVERPROCESS.

Test the pastry by pinching a piece between your fingers; if it is still crumbly add a little more water and pulse once or twice. Do not allow the pastry to form into a ball at this stage because the baked crust will become tough. Turn out the pastry on to a sheet of cling film.

3 Using the cling film as a guide, hold each side with one hand and gently push the pastry away from you, turning the pastry and holding the opposite sides of the cling film to contain it, until the pastry is smooth and just blended. Flatten the pastry into a disc and wrap with the cling film. Refrigerate for 1 hour or overnight.

For a Light Nut Crust add 25–40g/ 1–1½oz finely chopped nuts to the flour mixture before adding any liquid.

EXTRA SWEET PASTRY
(*Pâte Sucrée Riche*)

With a little more sugar and egg yolk, pastry becomes a melting, rich biscuit or shortbread pastry, that is ideal for encasing fruit tarts and tartlets. This pastry is very tricky to handle; although chilling is important, do not chill for too long or it will be too firm to roll out. If you cannot roll it out, simply press it in the tart tin using flour-dipped fingers.

Ingredients

- For a 23-cm/9-in tart tin

- 150g/5½oz plain flour
- ½ tsp salt
- 4–5 tbsp icing sugar
- 115g/4oz cold unsalted butter, cut into small pieces
- 3 egg yolks, beaten with 1 tbsp iced water and ½ tsp vanilla essence (optional)

Proceed as for Basic Sweet Pastry.

EASY NUT CRUST

This is a delicious flavourful crust, which makes an ideal base for custards and cooked fillings. It does not need rolling out and can be pressed straight into a tart tin with lightly floured hands, chilled and then baked without weighting with beans.

Ingredients

- For a 23-cm/9-in tart tin

- 225g/8oz unsalted butter at room temperature
- 1 egg, lightly beaten
- 1 tsp vanilla or almond essence (optional)
- 225g/8oz plain flour
- ½ tsp sugar
- 150g/5½oz walnuts, pecans, almonds, hazelnuts or
  macadamia nuts, finely chopped

1 Lightly spray or brush the tart tin with a vegetable cooking spray or a little melted butter or oil.
2 Using an electric mixer, cream the butter in a large bowl. Add the egg and vanilla essence and beat until blended. Sprinkle over the flour, sugar and nuts and beat on low speed until well blended.
3 Scrape the mixture into the prepared tin and press evenly on to the bottom and up the side of the tart tin or pie plate. Using a fork, prick the bottom of the pastry. Place in a refrigerator and chill for at least 30 minutes.
4 Preheat the oven to 180°C/350°F/Gas 4. Bake for 20 minutes or until golden and set. Transfer to a wire rack to cool before filling.

CRUMB CRUST

This easy crumb crust, popular for cheese-cakes, is ideal for chilled tarts since it remains crisp and crunchy, and is particularly good for ice cream tarts and chilled chiffon mixtures. For alternative flavourings to suit different fillings, use vanilla, chocolate, Amaretti biscuits (about 24) or gingernuts (about 24–26 biscuits) instead of digestive biscuits, or replace 50g/1¾oz of the crumbs with 75g/2¾oz finely chopped nuts for a Nut Crumb Crust.

Ingredients

- For a 23-cm/9-in tart tin

- 150g/5½oz digestive biscuits (18–20 biscuits) or other biscuit crumbs
- 90g/3oz butter or margarine, melted
- 1–2 tbsp sugar, or to taste

1 If making your own crumbs, put the digestive biscuits or alternatives in the bowl of a food processor fitted with the metal blade and process for 20–30 seconds until fine crumbs form. Alternatively, put them in a heavy-duty freezer bag and press into fine crumbs with a rolling pin. Pour them into a bowl and stir in the melted butter or margarine and sugar, if using. Pour into a tart tin and press crumbs on to the bottom and up the side of tart tin or pie plate. Chill, uncovered, for at least 20 minutes in the refrigerator.
2 Preheat the oven to 190°C/375°F/Gas 5. Bake the crust 6–8 minutes until set. Remove to a wire rack to cool. It must be completely cool before filling.

CREAM CHEESE PASTRY

Cream cheese pastry is a moist, flaky pastry often used with sugary or nutty fillings. It is ideal for rich tartlets and tiny petit fours.

Ingredients

- For a 23-cm/9-in tart tin or twelve 2.5–7-cm/2–3-in tartlet tins

- 150g/5½oz plain flour
- ½ tsp salt
- 1 tsp sugar
- 115g/4oz unsalted butter, at room temperature
- 115g/4 oz full-fat soft cheese, at room temperature

1 In a large bowl, sift together the flour and salt. Add the butter and soft cheese and, with an electric mixer, beat the ingredients together until well blended and a soft pastry forms. Shape into a ball, flatten to a disc and wrap tightly. Refrigerate about 1 hour before rolling and shaping.

RICH CHEESE PASTRY

This pastry is based on a Rich Shortcrust Pastry and makes a rich, flavourful alternative pastry for savoury tarts. It complements tomato-based fillings. Use a grated hard cheese, such as Cheddar.

Ingredients

- For a 25-cm/10-in tart tin

- 180g/6¼oz plain flour
- ¼ tsp salt
- ⅛ tsp cayenne pepper

- ½ tsp dry mustard
- 90g/3oz cold unsalted butter, cut into small pieces
- 2 tbsp cold white vegetable fat, cut into small pieces
- 60g/2oz mature Cheddar cheese, grated
- 1 egg yolk beaten with 2 tbsp iced water

Proceed as for Rich Shortcrust Pastry, adding the cheese after the butter and white vegetable fat are cut in, and mix well to combine.

CHOCOLATE PASTRY

This is a wonderfully rich, sweet pastry, almost like a chocolate biscuit. It makes a stunning background for fruit tarts and tartlets, as well as chocolate fillings.

Ingredients
- For a 23–25-cm/9–10-in tart tin

- 115g/4oz unsalted butter, softened
- 70g/2¾oz caster sugar
- ½ tsp salt
- 2 tsp vanilla essence
- 40g/1½oz cocoa powder (preferably Dutch processed)
- 180g/6¼oz plain flour

1 Put the butter, sugar, salt and vanilla into the bowl of a food processor fitted with the metal blade and process for 25–30 seconds until creamy, scraping down the sides of the bowl when necessary. Add the cocoa and process about 1 minute, until well blended. Add the flour all at once and, using the pulse button, process for 10–15 seconds until the flour is well blended. Scrape the pastry

out on to a sheet of cling film and shape into a flat circle. Wrap and refrigerate.
2 Soften the pastry for 10–15 minutes at room temperature. Unwrap the pastry and sandwich between two large pieces of cling film. Carefully roll out to about a 27.5-cm/11-in round, about 0.5cm/¼in thick. Peel off the top sheet and invert the pastry into a greased tart tin. Gently ease the pastry on to the bottom and sides of the tin, then remove the bottom layer of cling film. Press the pastry on to the bottom and sides of the tin, then roll the rolling pin over the top of the tin to cut off any excess pastry. Prick the base of the pastry with a fork and refrigerate 1 hour.
3 Preheat the oven to 200°C/400°F/Gas 6. Blind bake for 10 minutes. Remove the paper or foil and beans and continue baking for 5 more minutes until just set. Transfer to a wire rack to cool completely.

TIPS FOR FILLING TARTS

- For easier handling, and to avoid any overflows, always set tart tin on a heavy baking sheet.
- Beat the eggs and milk or cream mixture in a large measuring cup or pitcher, rather than a bowl, since it will be easier to pour.
- To fill the tart case with a liquid filling, set the tart on a baking sheet. Pull out the middle oven rack halfway and set the tart on its baking sheet on the rack. Pour in as much filling as possible and gently slide the rack back in place. Bake 5 minutes as this allows a thin crust to form over the top. If any mixture remains, pull the oven rack out and carefully pour the remaining

mixture into the centre of the tart. Slide the rack back in place.
- To remove the side of the tart tin, set the tart tin bottom on a sturdy can and allow the side to drop down gently on to the surface, leaving the tart on the bottom of the tin. Slide on to a serving plate.
- For a savoury tart, sprinkle cheese over the partially baked tart case to keep the pastry from getting soggy. When the cheese melts it forms a barrier between the pastry and the filling.
- Rubbing an unbaked tart case with 15g/½oz of softened butter and chilling before filling helps prevent a soggy crust.
- Brushing a warm, baked blind tart case with a little beaten egg or egg white and returning it to the oven for 2 minutes, creates a seal between the pastry and the filling, preventing a soggy crust. Brushing a baked tart case with melted preserves helps prevent a fruit-filled tart from becoming soggy.
- There are many tart tins on the market. Use a dull metal or non-stick tin as they produce the most well-cooked, crisp pastry. Shiny metal reflects heat, and glass and china absorb it, preventing the pastry from browning well. A trick I use to present or transport a tart is this: bake the tart in a metal, removeable-bottomed tin. Remove the side of the tin from the baked tart, leaving it on the metal bottom, then slide into a quiche dish of the same size.
- To test if the filling is set, insert a sharp knife into the centre. It should come out clean and should feel hot to the touch.
- If the pastry edge begins to brown before the filling is set, cover with foil.

chapter two

FROM THE OCEANS TO THE PRAIRIES

SMOKED SALMON, CREAMY LEEK AND ORANGE TART

A hint of orange rind brings out the flavour of the leeks and smoked salmon.

● Preheat the oven to 190°C/375°F/ Gas 5. Put the leeks, whipping cream and orange rind into a medium saucepan. Set over a medium-high heat and bring to the boil. Simmer until the leeks are tender and cream reduced to a thick purée consistency. Remove from the heat and stir in the chives or dill and season with pepper. Spread evenly on the bottom of the tart case.

● Arrange the smoked salmon strips evenly over the leek mixture. Set on a baking sheet for easier handling.
● Beat the sour cream or crème fraîche, egg and egg yolk and pour over the leeks and smoked salmon strips. Bake until the filling is set and golden, about 25 minutes. Transfer to a wire rack to cool slightly. Serve warm or at room temperature.

. . . .
● 23-cm/9-in tart tin lined with Rich Shortcrust Pastry *(Pâte Brisée Riche)*, partially baked blind

● 3 leeks, trimmed, washed and cut into 0.5-cm/¼-in slices
● 225ml/8fl oz whipping cream
● grated rind of ½ orange
● 2 tbsp chopped fresh chives or dill
● freshly ground black pepper
● 225g/8oz smoked salmon, cut into thin strips
● 3 tbsp sour cream or crème fraîche
● 1 egg
● 1 egg yolk
. . . .

CHEESY HAM AND BROCCOLI TART

....
- 20 x 30-cm/8 x 12-in rectangular tart tin lined with Cheese Pastry, partially baked blind

- 300g/10½oz broccoli florets, blanched
- 225g/8oz cooked ham, cut into1-cm/½-in pieces
- 350ml/4fl oz whipping cream
- 125ml/4fl oz milk
- 3 eggs
- 2 egg yolks
- salt
- freshly ground black pepper
- 150g/5½oz Gruyère or Emmenthal cheese, grated

....

The classic flavours of ham and cheese marry well with broccoli.

- Preheat the oven to 190°C/375°F/Gas 5. Arrange the blanched broccoli evenly over the bottom of the tart case, then sprinkle over the ham pieces or slices.

- Beat the cream, milk, eggs and egg yolks until well blended. Season with salt and pepper and stir in the cheese. Pour over the filling. Bake until set and golden, 30–35 minutes. Transfer to a wire rack to cool slightly. Serve hot or warm.

ROASTED SALMON AND SPRING ONION TART

....
- 20 cm/8-in square tart tin lined with 225g/8oz ready-made puff pastry, baked blind

- 450g/1lb fresh salmon fillet
- 1 tbsp olive oil
- 25g/1oz butter
- 4–6 spring onions, cut into 5-cm/2-in pieces
- 50ml/2fl oz sour cream
- 2 tbsp chopped fresh chives
- salt
- freshly ground black pepper
- 25g/1oz chopped nuts mixed with 15g/½oz dried breadcrumbs

....

This tart can be made with leftover poached salmon, but the oven roasting gives the fish a more pronounced flavour.

- Preheat the oven to 220°C/425°F/Gas 7. Line a small roasting tin with foil. Put the salmon fillet in the pan and brush with the oil. Roast until the fish is golden and just opaque, 10–12 minutes. Transfer to a wire rack to cool slightly.
- In a medium frying pan over a medium-high heat, melt the butter. Add the spring onions and cook, stirring frequently, until lightly coloured. Stir in the sour cream until blended and season with salt and pepper. Remove from the heat.

- Using a fork, flake the fish into fairly large pieces and stir into the spring onion mixture, tossing to blend. Spread in the tart case and sprinkle with the nut-breadcrumb mixture. Return to the oven for 2–3 minutes, until the top is crisp and tart is heated through. Serve immediately.

CRAB AND RED PEPPER TARTLETS

. . . .
- 4 sheets phyllo pastry, defrosted if frozen

- 60–75g/2–2¾oz butter, melted
- 3 red peppers, seeded and cut lengthways into thin strips
- 1 tbsp chopped dill
- 60g/2oz Parmesan cheese, freshly grated
- 225g/8oz fresh white crabmeat
- 2 tbsp mayonnaise
- 1 tbsp lemon or lime juice
. . . .

Buy good quality fresh white crabmeat for these delicate tartlets. Use a mini-muffin tin to make hors d'oeuvre-size tartlets.

- In a large frying pan over a medium heat, melt 25g/1oz of the butter. Add the red pepper strips and cook until softened. Remove from the heat and stir in the dill.
- Preheat the oven to 180°C/350°F/Gas 4. Lightly grease eight 5.5 x 2cm/2½ x 1¼in muffin tin cups. Stack the phyllo pastry sheets on a work surface and cut into 10–12.5cm/4–5in squares.
- Place one square on the work surface and brush lightly with a little butter; do not brush right up to the edge. Sprinkle with a little Parmesan cheese. Place a second square on top of the first at a right angle, to create a star shape. Brush lightly with butter and sprinkle with a little Parmesan. Top with a third square, at an angle to the first two, but do not brush with butter. Ease into one of the muffin tin cups, keeping the edges pointing up to form a flat-bottomed tulip shape. (Keep the phyllo pastry sheets you aren't working with covered with a damp tea-towel to prevent them from drying out.) Line the remaining cups.
- Bake until crisp and golden, about 10 minutes. Transfer to a wire rack to cool slightly. Carefully remove each phyllo case and set on a wire rack to cool. Divide the pepper mixture evenly among the tartlet cases and top each with a little crabmeat. Mix the mayonnaise with the lemon or lime juice and drizzle a little sauce over the crabmeat. Garnish with dill sprigs.

CREAMY LOBSTER TARTLETS

. . . .
- 3–4 sheets phyllo pastry, defrosted if frozen

- 40–60g/1½–2oz butter, melted
- 60g/2oz Parmesan cheese, freshly grated
- 750g/1½lb cooked fresh lobster meat
- 250ml/8fl oz whipping cream
- 1 egg
- 1 egg yolk
- salt
- pinch of cayenne pepper
- freshly grated nutmeg
. . . .

This is an extravagant dish as it requires a good portion of lobster for each serving.

- Preheat the oven to 190°C/375°F/Gas 5. Lightly grease six 7.5-cm/3-in tartlet pans. Cut twenty-four 10-cm/4-in circles from the phyllo pastry.
- Place one round on the work surface and brush lightly with a little butter. Ease into one of the tartlet pans. Sprinkle with a little Parmesan cheese. Brush a second round with a little of the butter and layer over the first, sprinkle with a little cheese and top with a third pastry round. Keep the remaining phyllo pastry rounds covered with a damp tea towel to prevent the pastry from drying out. Line the remaining tartlet pans.
- Divide the lobster meat evenly among the lined tartlet cases. Beat the cream, egg and egg yolk until well blended. Season with salt, cayenne pepper and freshly grated nutmeg. Divide evenly among the tartlet cases and sprinkle each with any remaining cheese. Bake until the filling is set and the pastry crisp, about 15 minutes. Cool slightly and then serve.

SEAFOOD AND TOMATO CREAM TART

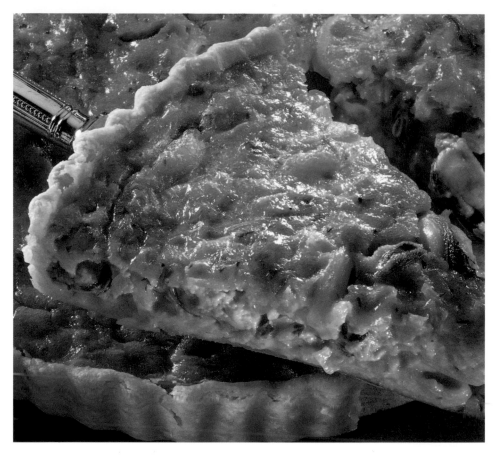

. . . .

• 23-cm/9-in tart tin lined with Rich Shortcrust Pastry (*Pâte Brisée Riche*), partially baked blind

• 15g/½oz butter
• 1 small onion, chopped
• 4 plum tomatoes, peeled, seeded and chopped
• 1 tbsp plain flour
• ½ tsp dried thyme
• 1 tbsp tomato purée
• 350ml/12fl oz whipping cream
• salt
• freshly ground black pepper
• 1 tbsp chopped fresh parsley
• 450g/1lb cooked mixed seafood or medium prawns, well drained
• 2 eggs

. . . .

This creamy tomato-flavoured custard makes a perfect base for prawns, or lobster, as well as mixed seafood.

● Preheat the oven to 190°C/375°F/Gas 5. In a medium saucepan over a medium heat, melt the butter. Add the onion and cook until just softened, 3–5 minutes. Stir in the chopped tomatoes, sprinkle in the flour and cook 1–2 more minutes.

● Add the thyme and tomato purée and whisk in the cream. Cook, stirring frequently, until the sauce is thickened and reduced by about one third. Season with salt and pepper and stir in the parsley. Remove from the heat to cool slightly.
● Spread the seafood evenly on the bottom of the tart case. Set on a baking sheet for easier handling. Beat the eggs into the tomato cream and pour over the seafood. Bake until set and golden, about 35 minutes. Serve warm or at room temperature.

PARMA HAM, FIG AND FONTINA BARQUETTES

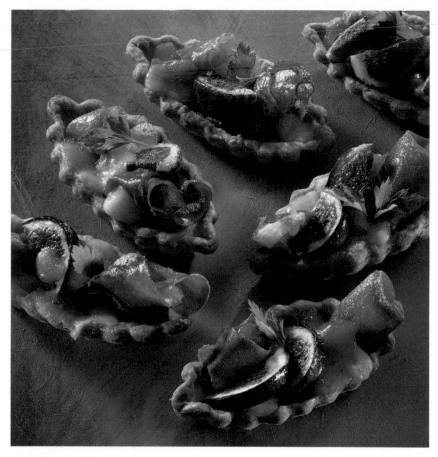

• 12 barquette moulds lined with Rich Shortcrust Pastry *(Pâte Brisée Riche)*, baked blind

• 12 slices Parma ham, trimmed, and cut in half lengthways
• 4 figs, halved and thinly sliced
• 150g/5½oz fontina cheese, diced
• freshly ground black pepper
• parsley or basil leaves for garnish

The saltiness of the Parma ham and sweetness of the figs are balanced by the fontina cheese to create a delicious pastry hors d'oeuvre. If you like, use to fill six 7.5-cm / 3-in tartlets and serve as a starter.

• Preheat the oven to 190°C/375°F/ Gas 5. Roll the Parma ham and fill the barquettes with fig slices and diced cheese and Parma ham rolls. Grind a little black pepper over each barquette. Set on a baking sheet for easier handling.
• Bake until the cheese is just melted and pastry heated through, 3–5 minutes. Serve hot or warm.

SPANISH TORTILLA TART

. . . .
- 23-cm/9-in tart tin lined with Rich Shortcrust Pastry (*Pâte Brisée Riche*), partially baked blind

- 1 tbsp olive oil
- 1 small onion, thinly sliced
- 1 red or green pepper, seeded and thinly sliced
- 2 garlic cloves, chopped
- 2–3 sun-dried tomatoes packed in oil, chopped
- 8–10 stoned black olives, chopped
- 1 large potato (about 225g/8oz), cooked and sliced
- 60g/2oz chorizo, cut into thin strips
- 2 tsp chopped canned jalapeño chillies
- 4 eggs
- 175ml/6fl oz milk
- 50ml/2fl oz whipping cream
- ½ tsp salt
- freshly ground black pepper
- ½ tsp paprika
- 75g/2¾oz Cheddar cheese, grated
. . . .

The pastry case creates a tender, flaky container for an omelette-like filling with typical Stinish-style flavours.

- Preheat the oven to 190°C/375°F/Gas 5. In a medium frying pan over a medium heat, heat the oil. Add the onion, pepper, and garlic and cook, stirring occasionally, until softened, about 8 minutes. Reserve one quarter of the mixture and spread the remainder evenly on the bottom of the tart case. Set on a baking sheet for easier handling.
- Sprinkle the onion mixture with three-quarters of the sun-dried tomatoes and olives, and arrange the potato slices over the top. Sprinkle over the remaining onion-pepper mixture, sun-dried tomatoes and olives.

- Beat the eggs, milk and cream. Season with salt, pepper, and the paprika, then stir in the cheese. Pour over the vegetable layers. Bake until set and golden, about 30 minutes. Transfer to a wire rack to cool slightly. Serve hot, warm or at room temperature.

QUICHE LORRAINE

. . . .
- 23-cm/9-in tart tin lined with Rich Shortcrust Pastry (*Pâte Brisée Riche*), partially baked blind

- 225g/8oz bacon, cut into 0.5-cm/½-in slices
- 350ml/12fl oz whipping cream
- 3 eggs
- 1 egg yolk
- ½ tsp salt
- freshly ground black pepper
- freshly grated nutmeg
. . . .

The authentic "quiche", which originates in the Lorraine region of France, is a custard-based tart containing bacon, cream and eggs, and is served as an hors d'oeuvre. Purists say only this tart can be called a quiche. If you like, add 150g/5½oz grated Gruyère to the custard mixture.

- Preheat the oven to 190°C/375°F/Gas 5. Set the tart case on a baking sheet for easier handling.

- Put the sliced bacon in a frying pan over a low heat. When the fat begins to melt, increase the heat to medium and fry, stirring occasionally, until crisp. Drain on kitchen paper, then sprinkle over the bottom of the tart case.
- Beat the cream and eggs until well blended. Season with salt and pepper and a little grated nutmeg. (Stir in the cheese, if using.) Pour into the tart case. Bake until the filling is set and golden, about 35 minutes. Transfer to a wire rack to cool slightly. Serve at room temperature.

PEPPERONI, TOMATO AND CHEESE GALETTE

- 350g/12oz puff pastry or Rich Shortcrust Pastry (Pâte Brisée Riche)

- 1 tbsp virgin olive oil, plus extra for drizzling
- 1 small onion, chopped
- 2 garlic cloves
- 400-g/14-oz can Italian-style tomatoes
- 1 tbsp tomato purée
- 1 tsp dried oregano
- salt
- freshly ground black pepper
- 115g/4oz thinly sliced pepperoni
- 150g/5½oz Mozzarella cheese, grated
- fresh oregano leaves for sprinkling and extra for garnish
- 40g/1½oz Parmesan cheese, freshly grated

Use commercial puff-pastry or Rich Short-crust Pastry for this tasty pizza-like tart.

- On a lightly floured surface, roll out the pastry to make a 25–27.5-cm/10–11-in round. Carefully slide the pastry on to a lightly floured baking sheet and prick the bottom all over. Refrigerate for 30 minutes.
- In a medium frying pan over medium-high heat, heat the oil. Add the onion and cook, stirring occasionally, until beginning to soften, about 3 minutes. Add the garlic and cook 1 more minute. Stir in the tomatoes, tomato purée and dried oregano. Cook until the sauce is thickened and reduced, 10–12 minutes. Season with salt and pepper. Remove from the heat to cool slightly.
- Preheat the oven to 200°C/400°F/Gas 6. Wrap a 25-cm/10-in dinner plate with foil and centre it over the pastry. Weight it with baking beans and bake blind for 10 minutes, turning the pastry halfway through the time. Remove the weights and plate and bake for 2 more minutes.
- Spread the cooled tomato sauce evenly over the pastry round to within 1cm/½in of the edge. Arrange the pepperoni slices evenly over the top and sprinkle with the mozzarella and a few oregano leaves. Spoon over the Parmesan cheese. Bake until the pastry is crisp and cheese is browned and bubbling, about 10 minutes. (If the top browns too quickly, cover with foil.)

KING PRAWN AND FENNEL TARTLETS

- Six 7.5-cm/3-in tartlet tins lined with Rich Shortcrust Pastry (Pâte Brisée Riche), baked blind

- 25g/1oz butter
- 2 large fennel bulbs, trimmed, quartered and thinly sliced
- 50ml/2fl oz whipping cream
- 1 tbsp Pernod or other anise-flavoured liqueur
- salt
- cayenne pepper
- 18 tiger prawns, peeled and de-veined
- 40g/1½oz Parmesan cheese, freshly grated
- dill sprigs for garnish

The slight anise flavour of the fennel goes well with most seafood. The Pernod is not essential but does enhance the flavour even more.

- Preheat the oven to 190°C/375°F/Gas 5. In a medium frying pan over a medium heat, melt 15g/½oz of the butter. Add the fennel and cook, stirring occasionally, until the fennel is tender. Stir in 25ml/1fl oz of the whipping cream, add the Pernod and season with the salt and cayenne. Cook for 2–3 more minutes until the fennel is glazed and the cream absorbed. Divide the mixture evenly between the tartlet cases.
- Add the remaining butter to the frying pan. Add the prawns and the remaining cream, and stir gently until coated and heated through.
- Arrange three prawns in each of the tartlet cases and sprinkle each with a little cheese. Bake for 5–7 minutes until the prawns are glazed and tartlets crisp and heated through. Garnish and serve immediately.

chapter three

VEGETABLE TARTS

SWEET GARLIC, THYME AND OLIVE TART

This strong flavoured tart is served with goat's cheese and basil on top – it makes a great talking point. Substitute rocket or watercress for basil if you like.

● In a small saucepan over a low heat, melt the butter. Add the garlic and thyme and cook, covered, for 15–20 minutes, stirring occasionally, until the garlic is soft. Remove from the heat to cool slightly. Squeeze the garlic from its skin and discard skins. Mash the pulp with the butter and thyme.

● Preheat the oven to 190°C/375°F/Gas 5. In a medium frying pan, heat 1 tablespoon of the olive oil.

Add the onion and cook, stirring frequently, until soft and translucent, about 10 minutes. Spread evenly over the bottom of the tart case.

● Beat the cream and eggs and stir in the garlic purée. Pour into the onion-filled tart case and sprinkle the olives over the top. Bake until just set and lightly coloured, about 30 minutes. Remove to a wire rack to cool slightly.

● In a small bowl, toss the diced feta cheese in the remaining olive oil with the chilli flakes. Arrange on the warm tart with the basil leaves or watercress or rocket. Serve immediately.

. . . .

● 20–23-cm/8–9-in tart tin lined with Rich Shortcrust Pastry (*Pâte Brisée Riche*), partially baked blind

● 30g/1oz butter
● 4–6 large young garlic cloves, unpeeled
● 2 tsp fresh thyme leaves, chopped, or 1 tsp dried thyme
● 2 tbsp extra-virgin olive oil
● 1 large sweet onion, thinly sliced
● 225ml/8fl oz whipping cream
● 2 eggs
● 150g/5½oz mixed good quality black and green olives, rinsed, stoned, and halved
● 60g/2oz feta cheese, diced
● ⅛ tsp dried chilli flakes
● handful fresh basil leaves or watercress or rocket

. . . .

FANCY ASPARAGUS TRANCHE

- 35 x 10-cm/14 x 4-in tart tin lined with Rich Cheese Pastry or Rich Shortcrust Pastry, partially baked blind

- 15g/½oz butter
- 450g/1lb thin asparagus tips, well washed
- 125ml/4fl oz heavy cream
- 2 eggs
- 1 egg yolk
- ½ tsp salt
- ¼ tsp cayenne pepper
- 3 tbsp freshly chopped dill or chives
- 2 tsp Dijon mustard

A tranche is a "slice" in French. This rectangular tart makes an elegant presentation, as well as being easy to slice.

● Preheat the oven to 180°C/350°F/ Gas 4. Set the tart case on a baking sheet for easier handling. In a large frying pan over a medium-high heat, melt the butter. Add the asparagus tips and cook, tossing gently until tender-crisp and brightly coloured, 1–2 minutes. Remove from the heat and cool slightly. Arrange the asparagus spears crossways and top to tail in the tart case.

● Beat the cream, eggs and egg yolk until well blended. Season with salt and cayenne pepper, then stir in the dill or chives and mustard. Pour into the tart case. Bake until set and golden, about 25 minutes. Transfer to a wire rack to cool slightly. Serve hot or warm.

CHERRY TOMATO AND BASIL TARTLETS

- Six 10-cm/4-in tartlet tins lined with Rich Shortcrust Pastry *(Pâte Brisée Riche)*, baked blind

- 24 cherry tomatoes
- 6–8 fresh basil leaves, shredded
- 3 eggs
- 300ml/10fl oz whipping cream
- salt
- freshly ground black pepper
- 75g/2¾oz Gruyère cheese, grated
- 1 tbsp fresh or bottled pesto sauce

Using fresh or bottled pesto sauce brings out the flavour of these easy-to-assemble tartlets.

● Preheat the oven to 180°C/350°F/Gas 4. Arrange the tartlets on a baking sheet for easier handling. Arrange eight cherry tomato halves, cut-side up, in each of the tartlet cases. Sprinkle evenly with the shredded basil leaves.

● Beat the eggs and cream until well blended. Season with salt and pepper and stir in the cheese and pesto sauce. Fill each of the tartlets. Bake until just set and golden, 25 minutes. Transfer the tartlets to a wire rack to cool. Serve warm and garnish with fresh basil leaves.

RED ONION TARTE TATIN

- 225g/8oz commercial puff pastry or Rich Shortcrust Pastry (*Pâte Brisée Riche*)

- 15g/½oz butter
- 1 tbsp olive oil
- 750g/1½lb red onions, halved lengthways
- ½ tsp dried thyme
- 1 tbsp brown sugar
- ½ tsp salt
- freshly ground black pepper
- 50ml/2fl oz water
- 1 tbsp balsamic vinegar

This savoury onion tart is based on the famous French tarte Tatin.

- On a lightly floured surface, roll out the pastry to a round about 25cm/10in and slightly thicker than 0.5cm/¼in. Slide on to a floured baking sheet and refrigerate.
- In a 23-cm/9-in ovenproof frying pan or flameproof casserole over a medium–high heat, melt the butter with the olive oil. Add the onion halves cut side down. Fill any spaces with extra chopped onion. Sprinkle with the thyme, brown sugar, salt and pepper. Cook, shaking the pan occasionally, until the onions begin to colour, 3–5 minutes.

- Preheat the oven to 220°C/425°F/Gas 7. Add the water and vinegar to the pan and reduce the heat to medium. Cook until the liquid has evaporated and onions are tender-crisp, about 5 minutes. Remove from the heat and cool slightly, 2–3 minutes.
- Slide the rolled-out pastry round over the onion-filled frying pan. Using a knife, carefully tuck the pastry inside the edge of the pan. Pierce in 2 or 3 places. Bake for 25–30 minutes until the pastry is golden.
- Transfer to a wire rack to cool about 3 minutes. Run a knife around the edge of the pan. Place a heatproof serving plate over the frying pan and, using oven mitts, carefully invert them together. Gently remove the frying pan.

SPINACH, CAMEMBERT AND PINE NUT SQUARE

. . . .
• 25-cm/10-in square tart tin lined with Rich Shortcrust Pastry (*Pâte Brisée Riche*), baked blind

• 25g/1oz butter
• 2 shallots, finely chopped
• 225g/8oz baby spinach, washed and dried
• 175g/6oz Camembert, brie or other semi-soft cheese, rind removed and cut into small pieces
• 50ml/2fl oz sour cream
• 2 eggs
• salt
• freshly grated nutmeg
• 25g/1oz pine nuts

. . . .

The Camembert and sour cream combine to create a rich creamy filling in this tart.

• Preheat the oven to 180°C/350°F/ Gas 4. Place the tart case on a baking sheet for easier handling. In a medium frying pan over a medium heat, melt 15g/1½oz of the butter. Add the shallots and cook, stirring often, until just softened, 3–5 minutes. Spread evenly over the bottom of the tart case.

• Melt the remaining butter in the same pan and add the spinach, stirring gently, until it wilts, about 1 minute. Spread over the bottom of the tart case and sprinkle the cut-up cheese over the spinach.

• Beat the sour cream and eggs until well-blended. Season with salt and nutmeg and pour into the tart case. Sprinkle over the pine nuts. Bake until set and golden, 20–25 minutes. Transfer to a wire rack to cool slightly; serve immediately.

ARTICHOKE, ROCKET AND CAPER TART

- 25-cm/10-in tart tin lined with 350g/12oz ready-made puff pastry, partially baked blind

- 25g/1oz butter or 2 tablespoons olive oil
- 60g/2oz fresh rocket, washed, drained and coarsely chopped
- 400-g/14-oz can artichoke hearts or 8–10 frozen artichoke hearts, halved
- ½ tsp dried thyme
- salt
- freshly ground black pepper
- 2 tbsp capers, drained
- 2 tbsp raisins
- 225ml/8fl oz double cream
- 2 eggs
- 1 egg yolk
- 40g/1½oz fontina or Gruyère cheese, grated
- 25g/1oz hazelnuts, chopped (optional)

This tart uses ready-made puff pastry, but could be made with other shortcrust pastries or even phyllo pastry.

- Preheat the oven to 190°C/375°F/Gas 5. In a large frying pan over a medium-high heat, melt 15g/½oz butter or 1 tablespoon oil. Add the rocket and stir-fry until just wilted, about 1 minute. Spread evenly in the bottom of the tart case.
- Add the remaining butter or oil to the pan and stir in the artichoke halves. Sprinkle with the thyme and season with salt and pepper. Stir gently until just warmed through and seasoned, about 1 minute.

- Arrange the artichoke halves in an attractive pattern, cut side up, over the rocket. Sprinkle the capers and raisins evenly round the artichoke halves.
- Beat the cream with the eggs and egg yolk, if using. Season with salt and pepper and stir in the cheese and chopped nuts. Pour over the vegetables. Bake until set and golden, about 30 minutes. Transfer to a wire rack to cool slightly. Serve warm.

CHEESE SOUFFLÉ TART

- 23-cm/9-in tart tin lined with Rich Shortcrust Pastry (*Pâte Brisée Riche*), partially baked blind

- 25g/1oz Parmesan cheese, freshly grated
- 60g/2oz butter
- 1 small onion, finely chopped
- 4 tbsp plain flour
- 300ml/10fl oz milk
- 2 eggs, separated
- 1 tbsp Dijon mustard
- 150g/5oz Cheddar cheese, grated
- salt
- cayenne pepper
- 1 egg white

This cheese soufflé in a pastry case makes a great supper. For a special presentation, make individual tartlets but bake 10 minutes less.

- Preheat the oven to 220°C/425°F/Gas 7. Sprinkle the tart case with Parmesan cheese. Set on a baking sheet for easier handling.
- In a medium saucepan over a medium heat, melt the butter. Stir in the onion and cook for 1–2 minutes. Stir in the flour all at once and cook, stirring constantly, for 2 minutes. Gradually whisk in the milk, stirring until thick and smooth. Bring to the boil and cook for 1 minute. Remove from

the heat. Beat in the egg yolks, one at a time, then beat in the mustard and cheese. Season with a little salt and cayenne pepper. Set aside.
- In a medium bowl, with an electric mixer, beat all the egg whites with a pinch of salt until soft peaks form. Stir a spoonful of the whites into the cheese sauce to lighten it, then gently fold in the remaining whites and spoon the mixture into the tart case.
- Bake until the soufflé is puffed and golden, about 25 minutes. Serve immediately as you would a traditional soufflé.

SPICY MEXICALI TART

- 23-cm/9-in tart tin lined with Rich Shortcrust Pastry *(Pâte Brisée Riche)* or Rich Cheese Pastry

- 1 tbsp vegetable oil
- 2 onions, thinly sliced
- 1 small red pepper, seeded and thinly sliced
- 1 garlic clove, finely chopped
- 200-g/7-oz can whole kernel corn, drained
- 1–2 canned jalapeño chillies, chopped
- 300ml/10fl oz milk
- 4 eggs
- salt
- ½ tsp ground cumin
- 40g/1½oz Cheddar cheese, shredded
- 2 spring onions, finely chopped
- 1 tbsp chopped fresh coriander

The chopped chillies and Cheddar cheese give this tangy tart a Tex-Mex flavour. Monterey Jack is a mild flavoured semi-soft American cheese popular in Tex-Mex cooking. Mild Cheddar makes a good substitute. Adjust the amount of chillies to your own taste.

- Preheat the oven to 190°C/375°F/Gas 5. In a large frying pan over medium heat, heat the oil. Add the onions, red pepper, and garlic and cook, stirring occasionally, until softened, 7–10 minutes. Remove from heat. Stir in the corn kernels and chopped chillies and spread evenly in the bottom of the tart case. Set on a baking sheet for easier handling.

- Beat the milk and eggs until well blended. Season with salt and the cumin. Stir in the cheese, spring onions and coriander, then pour over the onion mixture. Bake until puffed and golden, about 35 minutes. Transfer to a wire rack to cool slightly. Serve immediately.

CREAMY POTATO TART

- 23-cm/9-in tart tin lined with Rich Shortcrust Pastry7 *(Pâte Brisée Riche)*, Rich Cheese Pastry, or Rich Herb Shortcrust Pastry, partially baked blind

- 4 large baking potatoes, unpeeled
- 25g/1oz butter, softened
- salt
- freshly ground black pepper
- ½ tsp dried thyme
- ½ tsp freshly chopped rosemary
- 175ml/6fl oz whipping cream
- freshly grated nutmeg

This potato tart makes an unusual accompaniment to roasted meats.

- Put the potatoes in a large saucepan with enough cold water to cover. Bring to the boil over a medium-high heat. Reduce the heat and simmer until the potatoes are tender. Cool under running cold water for about 5 minutes, then allow to cool completely.
- Preheat the oven to 190°C/375°F/Gas 5. Set the tart case on a baking sheet for easier handling. Peel the potatoes and carefully cut into very thin slices. Arrange a layer of overlapping potato slices on the bottom of the tart case and dot with a little softened butter. Sprinkle with salt and pepper. Continue layering with the potatoes and butter, and seasoning.
- Stir the herbs into the cream and season with a little more salt, pepper and grated nutmeg. Pour the cream over the potato layers, allowing it to seep between each layer. The cream should just come up to the top layer. Dot with the remaining butter.
- Bake the tart until the cream is absorbed and the top is golden and crisp, about 30 minutes. Transfer to a wire rack to cool slightly.

CHARGRILLED AUBERGINE AND PEPPER TART

• 23-cm/9-in tart tin lined with Rich Shortcrust Pastry *(Pâte Brisée Riche)* or Rich Cheese Pastry, partially baked blind

• 1 medium aubergine, thinly sliced crossways
• 2 courgettes, sliced diagonally crossways
• 60ml/2fl oz olive oil
• 1 red pepper, quartered and seeded
• 1 yellow pepper, quartered and seeded
• 1 large red onion, thickly sliced
• 115g/4oz soft goat's cheese, crumbled
• 125ml/4fl oz whipping cream
• 1 egg
• 1 egg yolk
• 25g/1oz Parmesan cheese, freshly grated
• ½ tsp dried oregano
• 1 tbsp tomato purée
• ¼ tsp dried chilli flakes

Grilling the vegetables before baking them in the tart really intensifies the flavours and brings out their sweetness.

● Preheat the grill. Line the grill pan with foil and arrange the aubergine and courgette slices in a single layer on the foil. Brush the surfaces generously with some of the olive oil. Grill the vegetables until just beginning to char, about 5 minutes. Turn and grill 5 more minutes. Arrange on the bottom of the tart case. Set on a baking sheet for easier handling.
● Arrange the red and yellow pepper quarters, skin-side up, with the onion rings on the foil and brush with the remaining oil. Grill until just beginning to char, 6–7 minutes. Remove any loosened skin and arrange them over the other vegetables in the tart case, distributing them evenly. Sprinkle the crumbled goat's cheese over the vegetables.
● Preheat the oven to 200°C/400°F/ Gas 6. Beat the cream with the egg and egg yolk. Stir in the Parmesan cheese, oregano, tomato purée and chilli flakes until well blended. Pour over the vegetables in the tart case. Bake until the filling is set and top is well coloured, about 25 minutes. Transfer to a wire rack to cool slightly. Serve warm.

TOMATO, MOZZARELLA AND PESTO TARTLETS

• Six 7.5-cm/3-in tart tins lined with Rich Shortcrust Pastry *(Pâte Brisée Riche)*, baked blind

• 4 tbsp fresh or bottled pesto sauce
• 175g/6oz mozzarella cheese, sliced
• 4–6 small Italian-style plum tomatoes, thinly sliced
• about 24 basil leaves
• 15g/½oz pine nuts

This combination of sweet-sharp tomatoes and creamy mozzarella is enhanced by a zingy pesto sauce.

● Preheat the oven to 200°C/400°F/ Gas 6. Spread the bottom of each tartlet case with a little pesto sauce. Arrange alternate slices of the cheese and tomato in an overlapping circle, tucking in 3–4 basil leaves between them, and sprinkle the surface with a few pine nuts.
● Set the tartlet cases on a baking sheet for easier handling. Bake until the cheese is softened and pine nuts just golden, 8–10 minutes. Serve immediately.

RED ONION AND BLACK OLIVE TARTLETS

. . . .

• • Six 7.5-cm/3-in tart tins lined with Rich
Shortcrust Pastry *(Pâte Brisée Riche)*, baked blind

• 90g/3oz Parmesan cheese, freshly grated
• 2–3 tbsp olive oil
• 4–5 large young garlic cloves, unpeeled
• 25g/1oz butter
• 3 red onions, thinly sliced
• ½ tsp dried thyme
• 2 tbsp whipping cream
• 1 tbsp chopped fresh parsley
• 18–24 good quality black olives, such as
Kalamata, stoned and halved

. . . .

The slight saltiness of the black olives makes a perfect contrast with the sweetness of the slowly cooked onions and garlic.

• Sprinkle each tartlet case with 15g/½oz of Parmesan cheese. Set on a baking sheet for easier handling.

• In a small saucepan over a low heat, heat the olive oil. Add the garlic and cook, covered, for 15–20 minutes, stirring frequently, until the garlic is soft. Remove from the heat and squeeze the garlic from their skins into a small bowl, mashing the flesh to blend.

• Preheat the oven to 190°C/375°F/ Gas 5. Meanwhile, melt the butter in a medium frying pan over a medium heat. Add the onions and cook, stirring frequently, until soft and translucent, about 10 minutes. Stir in the dried thyme and cream, and cook for 3–5 more minutes until all the liquid is absorbed and the onions are a purée-like consistency. Stir in the chopped parsley and reserved garlic purée.

• Carefully divide the onion mixture among the tartlet cases and sprinkle with the black olives. Bake until just heated through, about 5 minutes. Serve warm.

GORGONZOLA, PEAR AND PECAN TARTLETS

. . . .

• Six 7.5-cm/3-in tart tins lined with Rich Shortcrust Pastry *(Pâte Brisée Riche)*, enriched with 40g/1½oz chopped pecans or walnuts, baked blind

• 15g/½oz butter
• 2 medium dessert pears, peeled, cored and diced
• ¼ tsp dried thyme
• 1 shallot, finely chopped
• 180g/6¼oz Gorgonzola or other creamy blue cheese, crumbled
• 75g/2¾oz pecans or walnuts, coarsely chopped
• 150ml/5fl oz whipping cream
• 2 eggs
• pinch of cayenne pepper
• freshly grated nutmeg

. . . .

This may seem an unlikely combination but the contrasting flavours provide a delicious result.

● Preheat the oven to 190°C/375°F/Gas 5. Set the tartlet cases on a baking sheet for easier handling.
● In a medium frying pan over a medium-high heat, melt the butter. Add the pears and stir fry until well coated with the butter, 1–2 minutes. Sprinkle in the thyme and shallot and toss well, then cook for 1 more minute. Divide the mixture evenly among the tartlet cases, distributing the pieces evenly on the bottom of each.
● Distribute the cheese among the tartlet cases, spreading evenly. Sprinkle each with the chopped pecans or walnuts.
● Beat the cream and eggs until well blended and season with cayenne pepper and freshly grated nutmeg. Divide the mixture evenly among the tartlets. Bake until tops are golden and the cheese is melted, about 10 minutes. Transfer to a wire rack to cool slightly. Serve hot or warm.

SUN-DRIED TOMATO AND MOZZARELLA TART

- 1 recipe Rich Shortcrust Pastry (*Pâte Brisée Riche*)

- 175ml/6fl oz home-made thick tomato sauce or ready-made pizza topping
- 225g/8oz mozzarella cheese, shredded
- 4–5 large Italian-style plum tomatoes, sliced
- 6 sun-dried tomatoes, packed in oil, drained and sliced
- 225g/8oz smoked mozzarella cheese, sliced
- 6–8 fresh basil leaves, torn into small pieces plus extra for garnish
- virgin olive oil for drizzling
- freshly ground black pepper

Transform the idea of the classic tomato and cheese pizza by updating the ingredients and arranging them on a pastry base.

- Preheat the oven to 200°C/400°F/Gas 6. Roll out the pastry into a 27.5-cm/11-in round and use to line a 25-cm/10-in lightly greased pizza tray or shallow tart tin. Prick the bottom and blind bake for 10 minutes.
- Remove from the oven and prick the bottom again. Immediately spread the bottom evenly with the tomato sauce or pizza topping and sprinkle with the grated cheese. Return to the oven until the cheese just begins to melt, 3–5 minutes. Remove from the oven and cool slightly.

- Arrange the sliced tomatoes, sun-dried tomatoes and smoked mozzarella overlapping on the surface of the tart case in a decorative pattern. Sprinkle with the torn basil. Drizzle with about 1 tablespoon of olive oil and season with the pepper.
- Return to the oven until the pastry is golden and the cheese melted, and just beginning to colour, about 8 minutes. Serve, hot, drizzled with additional olive oil and garnish with fresh basil leaves.

YELLOW SQUASH AND PROVOLONE TART

- 23-cm/9-in tart tin lined with Rich Shortcrust Pastry (*Pâte Brisée Riche*), baked blind

- 1 tbsp olive oil
- 15g/½oz butter
- 300g/10oz yellow squash or courgettes, diced
- 1 small red pepper, diced
- ½ tsp salt
- freshly ground black pepper
- 2 tbsp bottled pesto sauce
- 225ml/8fl oz double cream
- 2 eggs
- 60g/2oz Provolone cheese, preferably aged, grated

If yellow squash is hard to find or out of season, simply use young courgettes.

- Preheat the oven to 190°C/375°F/Gas 5. Set the tart case on a baking sheet for easier handling.
- In a large frying pan over a medium-high heat, heat the oil and butter. Add the yellow squash or courgettes and red pepper and cook, stirring frequently, until just beginning to soften, about 5 minutes. Season with salt and pepper and spread on to the bottom of the tart case. Drizzle the surface with the pesto sauce.

- Beat the cream and eggs until blended. Stir in the grated cheese and pour over the filled tart case. Bake until set and golden, about 35 minutes. Transfer to a wire rack to cool slightly. Serve hot or warm.

RED PEPPER AND COURGETTE RIBBON TART

. . . .

- 23-cm/9-in tart tin lined with Rich Shortcrust Pastry (*Pâte Brisée Riche*) or Rich Cheese Pastry, partially baked blind

- 25g/1oz butter
- 1 tbsp olive oil
- 2 large red peppers, seeded and diced
- 1 plum tomato, seeded and chopped
- 1 tsp sugar
- salt
- freshly ground black pepper
- 4 courgettes, washed, dried and trimmed
- 225ml/8fl oz milk
- 2 eggs
- 75g/2¾oz Cheddar cheese, grated
- ½ tsp salt
- freshly grated nutmeg

. . . .

This tart makes an ideal light lunch and can be made with other sweet peppers such as yellow or orange. Use yellow squash, instead of courgettes, when available.

● In a medium frying pan over a medium heat, melt 15g/½oz of the butter and the olive oil. Add the peppers and tomato and cook, stirring occasionally, until softened and any liquid is evaporated, 10–12 minutes. Stir in the sugar and season with salt and pepper. Spread the mixture evenly on to the bottom of the tart case.

● Preheat the oven to 180°C/350°F/ Gas 4. Using a swivel-bladed vegetable peeler, peel each courgette lengthways into "ribbons". In a large frying pan, melt the remaining butter over a medium-high heat. Add the courgette ribbons and toss, stirring, until they just begin to soften, about 1 minute. Remove from the heat to cool slightly. Arrange the ribbons over the pepper mixture.

● Beat the milk, eggs and cheese and season with the salt, pepper, and a little grated nutmeg. Pour into the tart case. Bake until the filling is set and the pastry golden, about 25 minutes. Transfer to a wire rack to cool slightly. Serve hot, warm or at room temperature.

BROCCOLI, CREAM CHEESE AND PINE NUT TART

. . . .

- 23-cm/9-in tart tin lined with Light Wholemeal Pastry, partially baked blind

- 225g/8oz broccoli florets
- 175g/6oz full-fat soft cheese or soft cheese with garlic and herbs, softened
- 175ml/6fl oz double cream
- 3 eggs
- 1 egg yolk
- salt
- freshly ground black pepper
- 4 spring onions, finely chopped
- 1–2 tbsp freshly chopped parsley or dill
- 25g/1oz pine nuts

. . . .

For a hint of garlic and herbs, replace the plain full-fat soft cheese with a soft cheese with garlic and herbs, or add your own.

● Preheat the oven to 190°C/375°F/Gas 5. Bring a medium saucepan half filled with water to the boil. Drop in the broccoli and bring back to the boil, then cook for 3–4 minutes. Drain and rinse under running cold water; drain and pat dry. Arrange the broccoli evenly over the bottom of the tart case. Set on a baking sheet for easier handling.

● Beat the cheese until smooth. Gradually beat in the cream, eggs and egg yolk. Season with salt and pepper. Stir in the spring onions and parsley or dill and pour into the tart case.

● Sprinkle the pine nuts over the top. Bake until set and golden, about 35 minutes. Transfer to a wire rack to cool slightly. Serve warm.

chapter four

FRUIT AND NUT TARTS

RUSTIC STRAWBERRY RHUBARB TART

The classic strawberry-rhuberb combination is an ideal filling for an easy-to-make tart. It is also excellent made with apples and blackberries.

● Lightly spray or oil a large baking sheet. On a lightly floured surface, roll out the pastry to a 32.5–35-cm/13–14-in round; it doesn't matter if the shape is not perfect or if the edges tear, as this is a rustic tart. Slide on to the baking sheet and refrigerate 30 minutes.

● In a large frying pan over a high heat, melt the butter. Add the rhubarb and stir-fry until the juices begin to run and it just begins to lose its colour. Sprinkle in 3–4 tablespoons sugar and the flour and toss to coat. Remove from the heat and add the strawberries, tossing lightly to combine. Cool for about 5 minutes.

● Preheat the oven to 200°C/400°F/ Gas 6. Remove the pastry round from the refrigerator to soften for about 5 minutes. Sprinkle the surface of the pastry with the toasted or dried breadcrumbs and spoon the fruit on to the pastry to within 7.5–10cm/3–4in of the border.

● Using your fingertips, fold and crimp the wide border of the pastry over the fruit towards the centre. Sprinkle with a little sugar. It doesn't matter if the pastry cracks or is uneven, just pinch it together. Bake until the pastry is crisp and golden and fruit is bubbling, 35–40 minutes. Transfer the tart on its baking sheet to a wire rack to cool slightly. Serve hot or warm.

. . . .
● 1 recipe Basic Sweet Pastry *(Pâte Sucrée)* or Extra Sweet Pastry *(Pâte Sucrée Riche)*

● 15g/½oz butter
● 450g/1lb rhubarb, cut into 2.5-cm/1-in pieces
● sugar
● 25g/1oz plain flour
● 450g/1lb strawberries, hulled and halved if large
● 15g/½oz fresh breadcrumbs, toasted, or 25g/1oz home-made dried breadcrumbs
. . . .

CHOCOLATE BANOFFEE TART

. . . .

- 23-cm/9-in deep tart tin lined with Chocolate Pastry or Chocolate or Ginger Crumb Crust, baked blind

- 2 x 400-g/14-oz cans sweetened condensed milk
- 175g/6oz good-quality dark chocolate, chopped
- 150ml/5fl oz whipping cream
- 1 tbsp golden syrup
- 3 ripe bananas

WHITE CHOCOLATE WHIPPED CREAM
- 400ml/14fl oz whipping cream
- 150g/5½oz good-quality white chocolate, grated
- ½ tsp vanilla essence
- cocoa powder, for dusting

. . . .

Banoffee pie is an all-time favourite. Covering it with white chocolate whipped cream sends it right over the top. The toffee layer can be made ahead, but don't add the bananas and cream more than a few hours before serving.

● Puncture each of the cans of milk (this prevents any possible explosion while cooking). Put them in a medium saucepan and add enough water to cover. Bring to the boil then reduce the heat and simmer, covered, for about 2 hours. Be sure to top up with water. (Some milk may leak but this does not matter.) Carefully remove tins from water and cool.

● In a medium saucepan over a medium-low heat, combine the chocolate, double cream, syrup and butter. Cook until smooth and melted, stirring constantly. Pour into the prepared crust and refrigerate until set, about 1 hour.

● Prepare the white chocolate whipped cream. In a small saucepan over a medium heat, bring 25ml/4fl oz of the cream to the boil. Remove from the heat and stir in the grated white chocolate all at once, stirring until completely smooth. Stir in the vanilla essence. Strain into a medium bowl and cool to room temperature.

● Scrape the condensed milk into a bowl. Whisk the thickened "toffee" until smooth. Immediately spread evenly over the chocolate layer in the tart case.

● Slice the bananas thinly and arrange them in overlapping concentric circles over the toffee layer in the tart case. In a medium bowl, whisk the remaining cream until stiff peaks form. Fold a spoonful into the white chocolate cream to lighten it, then fold in the remaining cream. Spoon over the banana layer and spread to the edge. Dust the top with cocoa if you like. Refrigerate until ready to serve.

LAVENDER-SCENTED APPLE TART

. . . .
- 25-cm/10-in tart tin lined with Basic Sweet Pastry *(Pâte Sucrée)*

- 4 large Gala or Golden Delicious apples
- 125ml/4fl oz pineaux des Charentes or other sweet dessert wine
- 40g/1½oz granulated sugar

GLAZE
- 90g/3oz honey
- 1 tsp dried lavender or to taste

. . . .

The heady scent of lavender in this tart evokes the hills of Provence in France. Use fresh lavender if you can find it, or substitute rosemary or thyme for an equally intriguing flavour. For a pretty effect, do not peel the apples, but core and thinly slice them. The peel on the edge gives the cooked tart a colourful finish.

- Preheat the oven to 200°C/400°F/ Gas 6. Using a swivel-bladed vegetable peeler, peel the apples, then halve and core them. Place cut-side down on a work surface and cut crossways into thin slices. Toss with 3–4 tablespoons of the wine and 25g/1oz of the sugar.

- Starting at the outside edge, arrange the apple slices in overlapping concentric circles in the tart case. Sprinkle with the remaining sugar. Bake until the apples are tender and the pastry crisp and golden, about 40 minutes. Transfer to a wire rack to cool slightly.
- In a small saucepan over a medium-high heat, simmer the remaining wine, honey and lavender until reduced by half, about 5 minutes. Carefully brush the hot glaze over the tart. Serve warm.

SOUTHERN PECAN TART

. . . .
- 23-cm/9-in tart tin lined with Basic Sweet Pastry *(Pâte Sucrée)* or Rich Shortcrust Pastry *(Pâte Brisée Riche)*

- 250g/9oz pecan halves
- 3 eggs
- 225g/8oz dark brown sugar
- 90g/3oz golden syrup
- grated rind and juice of ½ lemon
- 60g/2oz butter, melted
- vanilla essence

. . . .

This all-American classic pie looks stunning when baked in a tart tin. Serve warm with unsweetened whipped cream or sour cream or, of course, vanilla ice cream.

- Preheat the oven to 180°C/350°F/ Gas 4. Pick out about 100g/3½oz of perfect pecan halves and set aside. Coarsely chop the remaining nuts.
- Beat the eggs and sugar together until lightened. Beat in the golden syrup, grated lemon rind and juice, melted butter, vanilla essence and the chopped pecans. Pour into the tart case. Carefully set on to a baking sheet for easier handling.

- Arrange the perfect pecans in concentric circles on top of the egg-sugar mixture. Bake until the filling is set and slightly puffed and pecans are well coloured, about 40 minutes. Transfer to a wire rack to cool slightly.

PLUM CRUMBLE TARTS

. . . .

• Six 8-cm/3½-in tartlet tins, lined with Basic Sweet Pastry *(Pâte Sucrée)*, partially baked blind

CRUMBLE TOPPING
• 50g/1¾oz sugar
• 35g/1¼oz light or dark brown sugar
• 100g/3½oz plain flour
• 75g/2¾oz walnuts or pecans, chopped
• ½ tsp ground cinnamon
• 75g/2¾oz cold butter, cut into small pieces

FILLING
• 750g/1½lb plums
• 15g/½oz butter
• 25g/1oz sugar
• ½ tsp ground cinnamon
• lemon juice

. . . .

Almost any firm fruit can be substituted for the plums. The sharpness of the fruit contrasts perfectly with the sweet crumble topping.

• Prepare the crumble topping. Put the flour in a large bowl and sprinkle the pieces of butter over the top. Using a pastry blender, cut in the butter until the mixture resembles coarse crumbs. Do not over-blend or the topping will be too dense. Stir in the sugars, nuts and cinnamon until well blended. Refrigerate until ready to use.

• Preheat the oven to 200°C/400°F/ Gas 6. Halve the plums and, using a small spoon, remove the stones; chop coarsely. In a large frying pan over a medium-high heat, melt the butter. Add the plums and toss to coat. Sprinkle with the sugar and cinnamon, and cook for about 1 minute. Cool slightly.

• Divide the plum mixture equally among the tartlet cases and set them on a baking sheet for easier handling. Spoon the crumble mixture over the plums, mounding it generously. Bake for 15–20 minutes until the topping is crisp and golden. Transfer tartlets to a wire rack to cool. Serve warm with crème fraîche, if liked.

BLUEBERRY CUSTARD TART

. . . .

• 25-cm/10-in tart tin lined with Basic Sweet Pastry *(Pâte Sucrée)* or Extra Sweet Tart Pastry *(Pâte Sucrée Riche)*, partially baked blind

• 450g/1lb fresh blueberries
• 300ml/10fl oz whipping cream
• 3 eggs
• 50g/1¾oz sugar
• ½ tsp almond or vanilla essence (optional)
• 90g/3oz blueberry preserves or honey
• 1 tbsp water
• icing sugar for dusting

. . . .

This delicious tart combines fresh and cooked blueberries for maximum flavour.

• Preheat the oven to 180°C/350°F/ Gas 4. Set the tart case on a baking sheet for easier handling. Reserve a quarter of the blueberries and set aside. Spread the remaining berries on the bottom of the tart case.

• Beat the cream with the eggs and sugar until well blended. Stir in the almond or vanilla essence and carefully pour the custard mixture over the blueberries. Bake until a knife inserted 2.5cm/1in from the edge comes out clean, about 30 minutes. Transfer to a wire rack to cool and set completely, about 30 minutes.

• In a small saucepan over a medium heat, melt the preserves or honey with the water until smooth and bubbling. Drizzle over the remaining blueberries and toss to coat. Mound the berries on to the centre of the tart and dust with icing sugar. Serve warm or at room temperature.

PEAR AND CHOCOLATE CREAM TART

* 23-cm/9-in tart tin lined with Extra Sweet Shortcrust Pastry (Pâte Sucrée Riche) or Chocolate Pastry

* 115g/4oz dark chocolate, melted
* 225ml/8fl oz whipping cream
* 60g/2oz sugar
* 1 egg
* 1 egg yolk
* 1 tsp vanilla or almond essence
* 3 medium ripe pears

. . . .

Sweet ripe pears baked into a rich, chocolate, creamy custard are a heavenly combination.

● In a medium saucepan over a low heat, melt the chocolate, cream and 25g/1oz of the sugar, stirring frequently, until smooth. Remove from the heat and cool slightly. Beat in the egg, egg yolk, and vanilla essence and spread evenly in the tart case. Set on a baking sheet for easier handling.
● Preheat the oven to 190°C/375°F/ Gas 5. Using a swivel-bladed vegetable peeler, carefully peel the pears, then halve and core them. Put them on a work surface cut-side down and cut crossways into thin slices.

● Arrange the pears spoke fashion in the tart case and press gently with the heel of your hand to fan out the pear slices towards the centre. Tap the tart gently on the work surface to eliminate air bubbles.
● Bake for 10 minutes. Reduce the oven temperature to 180°C/350°F/Gas 4. Sprinkle the surface of the tart with the remaining sugar and bake until the custard is set and pears are tender and glazed, about 20 more minutes. Transfer to a wire rack to cool slightly. Serve warm.

CHERRY ALMOND TART

* 23-cm/9-in tart tin lined with Basic Sweet Pastry (Pâte Sucrée)

* 150g/5½oz dried tart cherries
* 125ml/4fl oz water
* 100g/3½oz blanched almonds
* 2 tbsp plain flour
* 90g/3oz unsalted butter, softened
* sugar (see recipe)
* ½ tsp almond essence
* 1 egg
* 1 egg yolk
* 300g/10½oz stoned fresh sweet cherries
* icing sugar for dusting

. . . .

In this tart, dried tart cherries, are combined with fresh cherries for maximum flavour.

● In a small saucepan, combine the dried cherries and water. Bring to the boil over a medium-high heat. Reduce the heat and simmer over a low heat until the water is absorbed and cherries are soft and plump, about 15 minutes. Cool completely.
● Preheat the oven to 200°C/400°F/ Gas 6. Put the almonds in a food processor fitted with a metal blade. Process until fine crumbs form. Add the flour and pulse to blend. Add the butter, 100g/3½oz sugar, the almond essence, the egg and egg yolk and process for 10–15 seconds until

smooth and creamy, scraping down the sides of the bowl once. Spread the mixture evenly in the tart case.
● In a bowl, combine the fresh cherries and plumped dried cherries and sprinkle with 2–3 tablespoons of the sugar (or to taste). Toss well and spoon over the almond mixture, distributing the cherries evenly.
● Bake for 15 minutes. Reduce the oven temperature to 180°C/350°F/Gas 4, sprinkle the surface with another teaspoon of sugar and continue baking until the filling is puffed and is golden, about 25 more minutes. Transfer to a wire rack to cool slightly. Serve warm or at room temperature.

TARTE TATIN

- 350g/12oz ready-made puff pastry or 1 recipe Basic Sweet Pastry (Pâte Sucrée)

- 10 large Golden Delicious apples
- juice of 1 lemon
- 90g/3oz unsalted butter
- 150g/5½oz sugar
- ¼ tsp ground cinnamon
- crème fraîche or sour cream, for serving

This classic French tart was made famous by two sisters in a small town in France called Solonge; now it is served all over the world. It is equally delicious made with pears.

● On a lightly floured surface, roll out the pastry into a 27.5-cm/11-in round, about 0.5-cm/¼-in thick. Slide on to a lightly floured baking sheet and refrigerate until needed.

● Using a swivel-bladed vegetable peeler, peel the apples, then halve and core them. Sprinkle the apples with a little lemon juice as you work, to prevent them from darkening.

● In a 25-cm/10-in heavy-based, ovenproof deep frying pan over a medium-high heat, melt the butter. Add the sugar and cinnamon, stirring occasionally, until the sugar dissolves. Cook, stirring occasionally, until the sugar is a rich golden caramel colour. Remove from the heat.

● Carefully arrange the apple halves, rounded side down, around the outside edge of the pan, pressing them together tightly. Press the remaining apple halves into the centre, squeezing them into a circle (remember the apples shrink as they cook). Be very careful not to touch the caramel as it is dangerously hot.

● Return the apple-filled pan to the heat and bring to the boil. Simmer until the apples begin to soften and the caramel darkens, about 20 minutes. Remove from the heat to cool slightly.

● Preheat the oven to 220°C/425°F/Gas 7. Remove the pastry round from the refrigerator and allow to soften slightly, about 5 minutes. Carefully slide the rolled-out pastry round over the apple-filled pan, centring the pastry over the apples. Using a knife, carefully tuck the overhanging dough inside the edge of the pan. Pierce the pastry in 2 or 3 places. Bake until golden, 25–30 minutes. Transfer to a wire rack to cool, about 5 minutes.

● Run a knife round the edge of the pan to release any pastry that might be stuck. Place a heatproof serving plate over the pan and, using oven mitts, carefully invert them together (unmould this tart over the sink in case the caramel runs out). Gently remove the pan, loosening any apple that may have stuck. Serve warm or at room temperature. Serve with crème fraîche or sour cream.

FIG AND CARAMELIZED WALNUT TART

· · · · · · ·

• 25-cm/10-in tart tin lined with Easy Nut Crust, partially baked blind

• 8–10 fresh firm ripe figs
• 25g/1oz butter
• 35g/1¼oz light brown sugar
• 125g/4½oz walnut halves
• 35g/1¼oz good quality honey
• 1–2 tbsp lemon juice
• thick Greek yogurt or sour cream for serving (optional)

· · · · · · ·

The flavours of figs and walnuts are emphasized further by the walnut crust. You can use a Basic Sweet Pastry (Pâte Sucrée) if you prefer.

• Preheat the oven to 200°C/400°F/ Gas 6. Quarter the figs and arrange them in concentric circles, cut-side up on the bottom of the tart. Bake until the figs just begin to soften, about 10 minutes. Transfer to a wire rack to cool slightly.

• In a medium frying pan over a medium-high heat, melt the butter with the sugar. Cook, stirring occasionally, until a golden caramel colour, 1–2 minutes. Add the walnuts and toss to coat, stirring constantly. Pour over the tart, tucking the walnuts between fig quarters.
• In a small saucepan over a medium heat, heat the honey and lemon juice and brush or drizzle over the tart, then allow to cool slightly. Serve warm with the Greek yogurt or sour cream if liked.

SUMMER BERRY TART ON HAZELNUT CRUST

. . . .
- 23-cm/9-in tart tin lined with Easy Nut Crust made with hazelnuts, baked blind

- 750g/1½lb mixed summer berries, such as strawberries, raspberries, loganberries, boysenberries, blueberries, red or black currants
- 100g/3½oz red currant or raspberry jam
- 2 tbsp raspberry-flavour liqueur
- mint leaves for garnish (optional)
. . . .

The nuttiness of the pastry goes beautifully with the sweetness of summer berries. If you like, substitute other favourite fruits cut into bite-sized pieces.

- Cut any large strawberries in half or quarters and put in a large bowl. Add the remaining fruit and toss just to combine.
- In a small saucepan over a medium heat, heat the jam with the liqueur until melted and smooth, stirring frequently. Drizzle over the fruit and shake the bowl to help lightly coat the fruit.

- Pour the fruit mixture into the tart case, gently distributing fruit evenly over surface and into edge. If you like, garnish with fresh mint leaves.

DRIED APRICOT AND AMARETTO CREAM TART

. . . .
- 23-cm/9-in tart tin lined with Extra Sweet Pastry (*Pâte Sucrée Riche*), partially baked blind

- 90g/3oz blanched almonds
- 75g/2¾oz sugar, or to taste
- 225g/8oz cream cheese, softened
- 90g/3oz butter, softened
- 2 eggs
- 4–5 tbsp Amaretto liqueur
- 225g/8oz ready-to-eat dried apricots, halved
- 2 tbsp apricot jam
. . . .

The flavour of dried apricots is more intense than fresh and they are always available. For a change, use a crumb crust made with half digestive biscuits and half crushed Amaretto biscuits.

- Preheat the oven to 190°C/375°F/ Gas 5. In a food processor fitted with the metal blade, process the almonds with half the sugar until very fine crumbs form. Add the remaining sugar, cream cheese, butter, eggs and 2 tablespoons of the Amaretto, and process until smooth and creamy, 20–30 seconds. Spread evenly on the bottom of the tart case. Set on a baking sheet for easier handling.

- Arrange the apricot halves over the filling, pressing them into the mixture, but not completely submerging them. Bake until the filling is set and golden, about 25 minutes. Transfer to a wire rack to cool slightly.
- In a small saucepan over a medium heat, heat the jam with the remaining liqueur until smooth and melted. Brush over the top of the tart. Serve warm.

STRAWBERRY HEART TART

- 300g/10oz ready-made puff pastry

- 750g/1½lb strawberries
- 150g/5½oz red currant jelly
- 2 tbsp Kirsch, cherry-flavour liqueur, or water (optional)

A heart-shaped cake pan can be used to make this tart, carefully unmoulding the pastry before filling. Alternatively, a free-form heart shape can be made on a baking sheet.

- Preheat the oven to 220°C/425°F/Gas 6. Lightly spray a 23cm/9in heart-shaped cake tin with vegetable oil. On a lightly floured surface, roll out the pastry to a circle about 0.3cm/⅛in thick. Line the cake pan with the pastry, pressing into the base. Trim and crimp the edges.
- Line the heart-shaped dough with foil and fill with beans. Bake blind for 10–15 minutes. Reduce the oven temperature to 200°C/400°F/Gas 6, remove foil and

beans and continue baking until crisp and golden brown, about 15 more minutes. Transfer to a wire rack to cool completely. Carefully remove the pastry heart from the pan.
- Cut off the stem end of the strawberries and slice each lengthways. If they have a rounded not pointed tip, cut them through the narrowest part to make them appear more pointed. Arrange them, tightly together, pointed ends up, in the tart case.
- In a small saucepan over a medium heat, heat the jelly with the liqueur or water until melted and bubbling. Cool slightly, then brush the berries with a thick layer of glaze, allowing it to dribble between the berries. Serve at room temperature.

SIMPLE ALMOND TART

- 25-cm/10-in square tart tin lined with Almond-Enriched Basic Sweet Pastry *(Pâte Sucrée)*, baked blind and still warm

- 90g/3oz unsalted butter, softened
- 100g/3½oz sugar
- 3 tbsp whipping cream
- 200g/7oz flaked blanched almonds, lightly toasted
- whipped cream or vanilla ice cream for serving

This tart is based on those made in Spain and Portugal, where white-blossomed almond trees cover the hills in the spring.

- Preheat the oven to 220°C/425°F/Gas 7 and line a large baking sheet with foil. With an electric mixer on high speed, beat the butter, sugar, and cream until light and fluffy, about 5 minutes. Gently fold in 150g/5½oz of the almonds and spread evenly over the bottom of the warm tart case; sprinkle with the remaining almonds. Set the tart on the baking sheet for easier handling.

- Bake the tart until the filling is bubbling and caramelized and the pastry is golden, 15–18 minutes. Transfer to a wire rack to cool completely (be careful since the caramelized filling is very hot). Serve at room temperature with whipped cream or ice cream.

MANGO GALETTES

- 1 recipe Extra Sweet Tart Pastry
(Pâte Sucrée Riche)

- 2 medium ripe mangoes
- 15g/½oz unsalted butter, melted
- 2 tbsp caster sugar
- 2 tbsp apricot preserves or honey

This idea can be used with any tender fruit which cooks quickly, such as nectarines, peaches or even papayas. Puff pastry also makes an easy-to-make base.

● On a lightly floured surface, roll out the pastry 0.5cm/¼in thick. Using a large fluted cutter or saucer as a guide, cut out six 10-cm/4-in rounds, re-rolling pastry scraps if necessary. Transfer to a large baking sheet, scallop the edges if you like and prick the bases to within 1.5cm/¾in of the edge. Refrigerate 30 minutes.

● Preheat the oven to 200°C/400°F/Gas 6. Peel the mangoes. Cut off each half and lay cut sides down. Slice thinly crossways.
● Arrange the mango slices over the pastry circles to within 1.5cm/¾in of the edge. Brush with a little melted butter and sprinkle each with a quarter of the sugar. Bake until the mango begins to caramelize and pastry is set and golden, about 15 minutes. Transfer to a wire rack to cool slightly.
● In a small saucepan over a medium heat, melt the apricot preserves or honey. Brush over the galettes and serve warm.

RASPBERRY 'N' CREAM TARTLETS

- Six 7.5-cm/3-in tartlet tins lined with Extra Sweet Tart Pastry (Pâte Sucrée Riche), baked blind

- 225ml/8fl oz milk
- ½ vanilla pod or 1 tsp vanilla essence
- 3 egg yolks
- 50g/1¾oz sugar
- 1 tbsp plain flour
- 1 tbsp cornflour
- 15g/½oz butter, diced
- 75g/2¾oz whipping cream (optional)
- 750g/1½lb raspberries
- 75g/2¾oz seedless raspberry jam
- 1 tbsp framboise or other raspberry-flavoured liqueur

This delicious pastry cream can be used as a base for any fruit tart. Do not assemble too far ahead as the pastry will soften.

● Pour all but 30ml/1fl oz milk into a medium saucepan. Split the vanilla pod and scrape the seeds into the milk with the bean. Bring to the boil over a medium heat and set aside to infuse for 15 minutes.
● Beat the egg yolks with the sugar until thick and light in colour, 3–4 minutes. Gently stir in the flour, cornflour, and the reserved 30ml/1fl oz milk to form a thick smooth paste.
● Remove the vanilla pod and bring the milk back to the boil. Slowly whisk into the egg mixture until well blended, then return the milk and egg mixture to the pan and cook, stirring constantly, over a

medium-low heat to thicken. Once thickened, increase the heat to medium-high and allow the custard to boil, about 2 minutes, stirring constantly. Scrape into a bowl and, if using vanilla extract, stir in at this point. Immediately sprinkle with the diced butter. Cool completely.
● If using the cream, beat until soft peaks form. Beat the cooled pastry cream to loosen it, then fold in the whipped cream. Spread a thick layer on the bottom of each tartlet case and cover with raspberries.
● In a small saucepan over a medium heat, heat the jam and liqueur until melted and bubbling. Brush or spoon lightly over the raspberries. These tartlets are best served at room temperature.

SUMMER FRUIT PIZZA TART

- 1 recipe Basic Sweet Pastry (*Pâte Sucrée*) or Walnut- or Almond-Enriched Basic Sweet Pastry

. . . .

- 2 tbsp honey
- 1 small peach, thinly sliced
- 1 small nectarine, thinly sliced
- 150g/5½oz strawberries, halved or quartered
- 60g/2oz raspberries
- 75g/2¾oz blackberries
- 75g/2¾oz blueberries
- 15g/½oz butter, melted
- 2–3 tbsp sugar

. . . .

This freeform tart resembles a pizza – cover it with any soft fruit you like. It's delicious with ice cream!

- Lightly spray or brush a large baking sheet with vegetable oil. On a lightly floured surface, roll out the pastry to an 27.5–30-cm/11–12-in round, about 1.3-cm/⅝-in thick. Transfer to the baking sheet. Crimp the edge and prick the bottom all over. Refrigerate for 30 minutes.
- Preheat the oven to 200°C/400°F/Gas 6. Line the pastry round with foil and weight with the bottom of a tart tin or ovenproof dinner plate. Bake 10 minutes until the pastry edge begins to colour. Remove the weight and foil.
- Gently brush the surface with the honey and arrange the fruits in triangles or circles over the surface of the pastry. Brush the fruit with the melted butter and sprinkle with the sugar.
- Bake until the fruit is tender and pastry is golden, 5–7 minutes. If you like, turn on the grill and grill the tart until the fruit begins to caramelize, 1–2 minutes. Cover the edge of the pastry with foil if it browns too quickly. Cool slightly and serve warm.

MINI-PINE NUT TARTLETS IN CREAM CHEESE PASTRY

. . . .

- 1 recipe Cream Cheese Pastry

- 1 egg
- 115g/4oz packed light to dark brown sugar
- 1 tbsp golden syrup
- 400g/1½oz unsalted butter, melted
- 150g/5½oz pine nuts, lightly toasted

. . . .

Cream cheese pastry has a lovely rich flavour and tender texture which goes beautifully with this sugary pine nut filling. Try pecans, walnuts or macadamias as well.

- Lightly spray or brush with vegetable oil one x 24-cup muffin pan. On a lightly floured surface, roll out the pastry 2cm/⅜in thick. Using a 6-cm/2½-in fluted cutter, cut out 24 rounds. Carefully line the muffin-pan cups, pressing the dough into the edge of each cup. Refrigerate for 30 minutes.

- Preheat the oven to 180°C/350°F/Gas 4. Beat the egg until foamy. Gradually beat in the brown sugar, golden syrup and melted butter. Stir in three-quarters of the pine nuts and carefully fill each muffin cup with the mixture. Sprinkle with the remaining pine nuts.
- Bake the tartlets until the filling is set and pastry edges are golden, about 20 minutes. Transfer the muffin pans to a wire rack to cool at least 20 minutes. Using the tip of a knife, loosen the pastry from each cup and unmould each tartlet. Serve at room temperature.

MACADAMIA TARTLETS

. . . .
- Twelve 8.5-cm/3½-in tartlet tins lined with Basic Sweet Pastry (*Pâte Sucrée*), partially baked blind

- 2 eggs
- 50g/2¾oz sugar
- 250g/9oz golden syrup
- 40g/1½oz butter, melted
- 3 tbsp whipping cream
- 1 tbsp orange-flavoured liqueur
- 40g/1½oz candied orange peel, chopped
- 250g/9oz unsalted macadamia nuts, coarsely chopped
- 115g/4oz plain or dark chocolate, melted (optional)
. . . .

These tartlets make a delicious dessert served with vanilla ice cream. Or, make them in tiny mini-tartlet moulds to serve with after-dinner coffee.

● Preheat the oven to 180°C/350°F/ Gas 4. Arrange the tartlets on a large baking sheet for easier handling.
● Whisk the eggs and sugar together until light and foamy, about 1 minute. Whisk in the syrup, butter, cream and liqueur, then stir in the orange peel and nuts.

● Divide the mixture evenly among the tartlets. Bake until the filling is set, about 20 minutes. Transfer to a wire rack to cool completely. If you like, drizzle or pipe each tartlet with a little melted chocolate. Serve at room temperature.

NECTARINE SHORTBREAD TART

SHORTBREAD PASTRY
- 225g/8oz plain flour
- 75g/2¾oz sugar
- ½ tsp ground cinnamon
- 115g/4oz butter, at room temperature, cut into small pieces

FILLING
- 750g/1½lb nectarines, stoned and sliced
- ½ tsp almond essence
- 25–40g/1–1½oz sugar
- 2 tbsp plain flour
- ½ tsp ground cinnamon
- 25g/1oz flaked almonds
. . . .

This tart uses a quick, shortbread-type pastry that does not need chilling or rolling. It is equally delicious topped with plums or peaches.

● Preheat the oven to 190°C/375°F/ Gas 5. Lightly spray or oil a 23-cm/9-in tart tin with a vegetable spray or oil.
● In a large bowl, stir together the flour, sugar and cinnamon. Sprinkle over the pieces of butter and, using a pastry blender, cut in the butter until a soft pastry begins to form. Turn into the tart tin and, using your fingertips, press the pastry evenly on to the bottom and up the side of the pan.

● In a bowl, toss the nectarine slices with the almond essence, sugar (to taste), flour and cinnamon. Starting at the outside edge, arrange the slices in overlapping concentric circles in the tart case. Sprinkle with the almonds.
● Set the tart case on a baking sheet for easier handling. Bake until the nectarines are tender and pastry is golden and crisp, 35–40 minutes. Rotate the tart halfway through cooking time if it begins to colour unevenly. Transfer to a wire rack to cool slightly. Serve warm, at room temperature or cool.

chapter five

CHOCOLATE, CUSTARD, AND CREAM TARTS

LEMON TART

This is one of my favourite tarts, a creamy sweet-sharp lemon filling encased in crisp tender pastry   simple but delicious.

● Preheat the oven to 190°C/375°F/ Gas 5. With an electric mixer on low speed, beat together the lemon rind, juice and sugar. Slowly beat in the cream or crème fraîche until blended, then beat in the eggs and yolks, one at a time.

● Set the tart case on a baking sheet for easier handling and carefully pour in the filling. (If you prefer a completely smooth filling, strain into the tart case, removing the rind.)

● Bake until the filling is just set, but not coloured, about 20 minutes. If the tart begins to colour, cover with foil. Transfer to a wire rack to cool completely. Dust with icing sugar before serving.

. . . .
● 23-cm/9-in tart tin lined with Extra Sweet Pastry *(Pâte Brisée Riche)*, partially baked blind

● grated rind of 2–3 lemons
● 150ml/5 fl oz freshly squeezed lemon juice
● 100g/3½oz sugar
● 125ml/4fl oz whipping cream or crème fraîche
● 3 eggs
● 3 egg yolks
● icing sugar for dusting
. . . .

LIME CURD PHYLLO TARTLETS WITH RASPBERRIES

- Four sheets phyllo pastry, defrosted if frozen
- 25g/1oz unsalted butter, melted
- sugar
- 2 eggs, beaten
- 115g/4oz unsalted butter, diced
- 100g/3½oz sugar
- 2 tbsp freshly grated lime rind
- 50ml/2fl oz freshly squeezed lime juice (1–2 limes)
- 450g/1lb fresh raspberries
- fresh mint sprigs for garnish (optional)

A delicious tangy lime curd makes an ideal filling for these crisp phyllo cups. The raspberries add a stunning colour, as well as flavour, contrast.

● Preheat the oven to 180°C/350°F/ Gas 4. Lightly oil four 175-ml/4-fl oz ramekins with vegetable oil. Cut the phyllo pastry sheets into 15-cm/6-in squares. Keep the phyllo pastry covered with a damp tea towel to prevent the pastry from drying out.

● Place a phyllo square on the work surface, brush with a little melted butter and sprinkle with a little sugar. Butter a second square and lay it over the first square at an angle; sprinkle with a little sugar. Repeat with two more phyllo squares. Press the stack of squares into a custard cup or ramekin, pressing into the edge and keeping the edges turned up. Continue to line the remaining ramekins.

● Set the cups on a baking sheet for easier handling. Bake until crisp and golden, about 10 minutes. Transfer to a wire rack and cool completely.

● In a medium saucepan, combine the eggs, butter, 100g/3½oz sugar and lime rind and juice. Cook over a medium-low heat until the mixture begins to thicken and bubbles begin to appear on the surface, about 3 minutes. Scrape into a bowl and cover with cling film, pressing the wrap against the surface of the curd to prevent a skin from forming. Refrigerate for at least 1 hour.

● Put half the raspberries and 2–3 tablespoons of sugar in a food processor fitted with the metal blade and process until smooth. Strain into a bowl and stir in the remaining berries. Divide the curd mixture evenly among the phyllo cups. Top each with some of the raspberry sauce; serve the remaining sauce separately. Garnish with mint.

DOUBLE CHOCOLATE TRUFFLE TARTS

- Eight 10-cm/4-in tartlet tins lined with Chocolate Pastry, baked blind
- 300ml/10fl oz whipping cream
- 300g/10½oz dark chocolate, chopped
- 25g/1oz unsalted butter
- 50ml/2fl oz Cognac, brandy, or other favourite liqueur
- cocoa powder for dusting

Rich and sophisticated, this makes an elegant dessert presentation.

● In a medium saucepan over a medium-high heat, bring the cream to the boil. Remove from the heat and add the chocolate, stirring until completely melted. Beat in the butter and stir in the Cognac or brandy. Strain the mixture into a measuring jug.

● Divide the mixture evenly among the tartlet cases, smoothing the tops so they are completely flat. Refrigerate for 3–4 hours or overnight.

● Cut out strips of greaseproof paper about 1cm/1½in wide. Place in a random pattern over a tartlet and dust with cocoa. Repeat with the remaining tartlets. Remove from the refrigerator about 15 minutes before serving.

PUMPKIN TART WITH PECAN PRALINE TOPPING

- 23-cm/9-in tart tin lined with Basic Sweet Pastry (*Pâte Sucrée*), partially baked blind

- 300g/10½oz canned solid-packed pumpkin
- 100g/3½oz sugar
- 50g/1¾oz packed light brown sugar
- 175ml/6fl oz whipping cream
- 75ml/2½fl oz milk
- 2 eggs
- 1–2 tbsp bourbon or whisky (optional)
- ¾ tsp ground cinnamon
- ½ tsp ground allspice
- ½ tsp ground ginger
- ¼ tsp ground cloves
- ¼ tsp grated nutmeg

TOPPING
- 60g/2oz pecans, chopped
- 110g/3½oz packed light brown sugar
- 25g/1oz unsalted butter, melted
- whipped cream or vanilla ice cream for serving

This is the traditional American Thanksgiving pumpkin pie with a face lift. The pecan topping is easy to make and adds a crunchy contrast to the creamy filling.

● Preheat the oven to 180°C/350°F/Gas 4. With an electric mixer, beat the pumpkin with the remaining ingredients (except the topping and whipped cream) until smooth and well blended. Set the tart on a baking sheet for easier handling and carefully pour the mixture into the tart case.

● Bake until the filling is just set (tart will continue to bake once removed) and pastry is golden, about 45 minutes. Cover the pastry edge with foil if it browns too quickly. Remove to a wire rack to cool completely, then refrigerate.

● Preheat the grill. Combine the pecans, sugar and butter, and sprinkle evenly over the tart. Cover the edge of the pastry with a strip of foil if necessary. Grill about 10cm/4in from the heat until the topping bubbles and caramelizes, watching carefully, about 1 minute. Allow to cool, then serve the tart at room temperature or chilled with whipped cream or ice cream if desired.

GINGERED CRÈME BRULÉE TARTLETS

These delicately flavoured tartlets will soon become one of your favourites. The thick custard can be flavoured by infusing the cream with a split vanilla pod if you prefer, but the ginger adds a subtle Eastern flavour.

● Preheat the oven to 160°C/325°F/ Gas 3. Set the tartlet cases on a baking sheet for easier handling.

● In a small saucepan over a medium heat, bring the cream to the boil. Whisk the egg and egg yolks with the sugar and ginger syrup until lightened, about 1 minute. Slowly whisk in the hot cream. Strain into a measuring jug and stir in the chopped ginger.

● Divide the mixture evenly among the tartlet cases. Bake until the custard is lightly set, about 15 minutes. Transfer to a wire rack to cool, then refrigerate for at least 4 hours or overnight.

● Just before serving, preheat the grill. Sprinkle a thin layer of sugar evenly over the custard right to the pastry edge. If the pastry is already very brown, protect with a thin strip of foil while grilling. Grill close to the heat until the sugar melts and begins to bubble, about 1 minute; do not over-grill or the custard will begin to curdle. Refrigerate immediately to allow the caramel to harden, about 5 minutes, then serve.

. . . .

● Four 10-cm/4-in tartlet tins lined with Basic Sweet Pastry *(Pâte Sucrée)* or Ginger Crumb Crust, baked blind

● 300ml/10fl oz whipping cream
● 1 egg
● 2 egg yolks
● 1 tbsp sugar
● 1 tbsp ginger syrup (from the bottle)
● 1 piece bottled stem ginger, finely chopped
● 60–90g/2–3oz golden granulated sugar

. . . .

CHOCOLATE GANACHE AND BERRY TART

- 23-cm/9-in tart tin lined with Chocolate Pastry, baked blind

- 650 ml/22fl oz whipping cream
- 300g/10½oz seedless raspberry jam
- 225g/8oz good quality dark chocolate, chopped
- 50ml/2fl oz framboise or other raspberry-flavoured liqueur
- 750g/1½lb mixed fresh summer berries, such as raspberries, blackberries, strawberries (quartered if large), loganberries or blueberries
- 1–2 tbsp caster sugar

Summer berries make a perfect match for a rich chocolate tart case filled with a dark chocolate and raspberry truffle mixture.

- In a medium saucepan over a medium heat, bring 400ml/14fl oz of the cream and three-quarters of the raspberry jam to the boil, whisking to dissolve the preserves. Remove from the heat and add the chocolate all at once, stirring until melted and smooth. Strain the mixture directly into the tart shell, lifting and turning the tart to distribute the filling evenly. Cool completely or refrigerate until set, at least 1 hour.

- In a small saucepan over a medium heat, heat the remaining raspberry preserves and 2 tablespoons of the framboise or other raspberry-flavoured liqueur until melted and bubbling. Drizzle over the berries and toss to coat well. Arrange the berries over the top of the tart. Refrigerate until ready to serve.
- Bring the tart to room temperature at least 30 minutes before serving. Whip the remaining cream with the sugar and remaining framboise- or raspberry-flavoured liqueur until soft peaks form. Spoon into a serving bowl and serve with the tart.

IRISH CREAM BARQUETTES

- 12 mini-barquettes or other mini-tartlet tins lined with Extra Sweet Pastry (*Pâte Sucrée Riche*), baked blind

- 115g/4oz plain chocolate, melted
- 125ml/4fl oz milk
- 3 egg yolks
- 25g/1oz sugar
- 3 tbsp plain flour
- 50ml/2fl oz Irish cream liqueur
- 50ml/2fl oz whipping cream, whipped
- chocolate shavings or cocoa powder for dusting

These little tartlets make an ideal accompaniment to an after-dinner coffee. Use other shapes to form the tartlets, such as hearts, squares or circles.

- Brush the bottom of each tartlet with a little melted chocolate. Set the tartlets on a baking sheet for easier handling.

- In a heavy-based saucepan over a medium heat, bring the milk just to the boil. Beat the egg yolks and sugar until light, about 1 minute, then stir in the flour. Add the hot milk, whisking constantly.
- Return the custard to the heat and cook, until it thickens, about 2 minutes, whisking constantly. Remove from the heat and whisk in the Irish cream liqueur. Allow to cool. Gently fold in the cream and refrigerate until thickened, about 30 minutes.
- Spoon the custard-cream into a piping bag fitted with a medium star nozzle. Pipe into the tartlet cases and refrigerate. Garnish with chocolate shavings or dust with cocoa just before serving.

CHOCOLATE SOUFFLÉ TARTS

· · · · · · ·
- 6–8 brioche moulds or other deep tartlet tins or ramekins, buttered and lined with Chocolate Pastry or Rich Shortcrust Pastry (Pâte Brisée Riche), baked blind

- 115g/4oz dark or plain chocolate, chopped
- 60g/2oz butter
- 4 eggs, separated
- 2 tbsp brandy or Cognac
- ¼ tsp cream of tartare
- 25g/1oz sugar
- icing sugar for dusting
· · · · · · ·

This recipe uses baked pastry cases to hold the soufflé mixture instead of ramekins. These baked cases can also be used to hold a mousse or other creamy tart fillings. If using chocolate pastry or other butter-rich pastry, leave the cases in the moulds as they will melt down when re-baked with the soufflé mixture.

- Preheat the oven to 220°C/425°F/Gas 7. Set the brioche-moulds or tartlet tins or ramekins on a baking sheet for easier handling.
- In a saucepan over a low heat, melt the chocolate and butter until smooth, stirring frequently. Remove from the heat and beat in the egg yolks, one at a time, then beat in the brandy. Set aside.
- In a large bowl and with an electric mixer, beat the egg whites and cream of tartare until soft peaks form. Sprinkle in the sugar, 1 tablespoon at a time, and continue beating until stiff peaks form.
- Stir a spoonful of whites into the chocolate mixture to lighten it, then fold in the remaining whites. Divide the mixture evenly among the tartlets, filling them almost to the pastry edge. Bake for 10–12 minutes until the mixture is just set, but still slightly wobbly. Dust with icing sugar and serve immediately.

MOCHA MOUSSE SLICE

· · · · · · ·
- 35 x 10-cm/14 x 4-in tart tin lined with Extra Sweet Pastry (Pâte Sucrée Riche) or Chocolate Pastry, baked blind

- 225g/8oz dark chocolate, chopped
- 50ml/2fl oz strong coffee
- 60g/2oz butter
- 2 tbsp coffee-flavoured liqueur or rum
- 3 eggs, separated
- ¼ tsp cream of tartare
- 25g/1oz white chocolate, melted, for decoration (optional)
· · · · · · ·

WARNING: contains uncooked egg whites.

A delicious way to serve a luscious chocolate mousse. For a special effect, decorate with white chocolate.

- In a medium saucepan over a medium-low heat, melt the chocolate and coffee until smooth, stirring frequently. Remove from the heat and beat in the butter and liqueur. Beat in the egg yolks, one at a time, until the mixture thickens.
- In a large bowl and with an electric mixer, beat the egg whites and cream of tartare until soft peaks form. Beat a large spoonful of whites into the chocolate mixture to lighten it, then fold in the remaining whites. Pour into the tart case.
- Make a paper cone: fold a square of greaseproof paper in half to form a triangle. With the middle triangle point facing you, fold the left corner down to the centre. Fold the right corner down and wrap completely round the left corner, forming a cone.
- Spoon the melted white chocolate into the cone and fold the top edge over to enclose it. Snip off the point of the cone to make a hole about 0.3cm/⅛in across. Pipe parallel lines of white chocolate crossways across the chocolate mousse surface. Using a wooden skewer draw across the white chocolate to feather the lines. Refrigerate for 2–3 hours or overnight to set competely.

ORANGE CARDAMOM TART

- 23-cm/9-in tart tin lined with Extra Sweet Pastry *(Pâte Sucrée Riche)*, partially baked blind

- 5 tbsp fine-cut orange marmalade
- sugar
- 300ml/10fl oz freshly squeezed orange juice, strained
- 2 large navel oranges, thinly sliced
- 115g/4oz unsalted butter, softened
- 2 eggs
- 2 egg yolks
- 150ml/5fl oz whipping cream
- seeds from 4–5 cardamom pods, lightly crushed
- grated rind of 3 oranges
- 40g/1½oz sultanas, plumped

This delicious orange tart is flavoured with cardamom seeds, which give it a slightly exotic touch. Topped with orange slices, it looks stunning.

- In a small saucepan over a low heat, heat 3 tablespoons of the marmalade until melted. Use to brush the bottom of the tart case with an even layer. Set on a baking sheet for easier handling.
- In a medium saucepan, combine 150g/5½oz sugar and 225ml/8fl oz of the orange juice. Bring to the boil and cook until thick and syrupy, about 10 minutes. Add the orange slices to the syrup and simmer gently until completely glazed, about 10 minutes. Carefully transfer to a rack set over a baking sheet to catch any drips. Reserve the syrup.

- Preheat the oven to 190°C/375°F/ Gas 5. With an electric mixer, beat the butter, eggs, egg yolks and 150g/5½oz sugar until lightened, about 2 minutes. Gradually beat in the cream, cardamom seeds and remaining marmalade. Stir in the orange rind, remaining juice and the sultanas. (The mixture may look curdled but it will be fine.)
- Pour the mixture into the tart case. Bake until the filling is just set, about 35 minutes. Transfer to a wire rack to cool slightly. Arrange the orange slices in overlapping concentric circles on top of the tart. Bring the reserved syrup to the boil and brush over the orange slices to glaze. Serve at room temperature.

FLORIDA KEY LIME TART

- 23-cm/9-in tart tin or pie plate lined with Ginger Crumb Crust

- 3 egg yolks, size 2
- 400-ml/14-fl oz can sweetened condensed milk
- 125ml/4fl oz Key lime or freshly squeezed lime juice (about 3 limes)
- 1 tbsp grated lime rind
- 225ml/8fl oz whipping cream

Originally made with the small, yellowish limes from the Florida Keys, this tart can be made with any limes. Florida key lime juice is available in bottles from larger supermarkets and some speciality stores.

- With an electric mixer, beat the egg yolks until thick and creamy, about 3 minutes. Gradually beat in the condensed milk, lime juice and rind. Pour into the tart case and refrigerate until completely set, for at least 4 hours or overnight.

- Beat the cream until stiff peaks form. Spoon the cream into a piping bag fitted with a medium star nozzle and pipe a decorative border between the outer edge and centre. Alternatively, serve cold with whipped cream passed separately.

WARNING: People with weak immune systems, or pregnant women may wish to avoid this dish because it contains uncooked eggs.